Amazon Income

How I Made Over $100K Selling Books On Amazon, Without Having To Write The Books Myself, And How You Can Do The Same

Chris Oberg

Contents

Introduction

This is no longer sustainable, I said out loud to myself one late summer evening in 2016. I had to find something else. Sure, my poker playing was generating a reasonably steady extra income on the side, but it came at a high price. Most of the favorable poker games were in the evening, the sessions were always several hours long and the financial fluctuations were starting to take their toll on me. I felt ready to put my cards on the shelf and try something new. And this time, it would be something that could generate money while I slept.

You may recognize the feeling I had that summer evening. The feeling that something is not quite right, that it's time to move on. It's often easy to put your finger on what doesn't feel quite right, but it's sometimes almost impossible to see a way out. "If I'm not going to have poker as a side income, what am I going to do?", I asked myself. It's much the same feeling as being stuck at a job you don't enjoy. It's obvious that the job is wrong, but how are you going to get out of it? You know you have to replace the job with another job, but which one?

Being stuck in something that is *good enough* not to be bad, whether it's a job, a relationship or a time-consuming poker game, is life's greatest enemy. It's like walking around with the handbrake half pulled. Life slowly rolls along, but it's with constant resistance and something shaking in the background.

That night, I started googling for other, for me, new ways to make money online. Most of all, I wanted to find a business model that could generate passive income - something I had previously only read about in economics books but which was always promoted as the holy grail of income. After a little bit of surfing on various sites, I came across the Canadian site *Project Life Mastery*. I was hooked right away. The impression I got from the site's owner, Stefan James, was that he was a cool guy and he also put into words many of my thoughts and concerns. He talked about how the way out of the spinning wheel, the way to financial freedom, was to stop trading your time for money. He talked about passive income. Bingo! That's exactly what I was looking for.

Stefan's model for generating passive income online was to publish and sell books on Amazon. That in itself wasn't particularly revolutionary, but what stood out was that he didn't write the books himself. He hired ghostwriters to write the books for him, for a one-off fee of a few hundred dollars per book. Stefan saw the books as digital assets, like a stock that generates dividends, and he published the books under fictitious author names. With this model, he got all the money from sales himself, in perpetuity. How clever!

Filled with energy and hope, the winds of change began to blow full force at home in my little poker office. I devoured all of Stefan's articles about selling ghostwritten books on Amazon and it wasn't many weeks before I had my first book of my own out there on Amazon. It was a book about time management. To say I was excited to try a new way of making money online was an understatement. I remember daydreaming about how much royalties that book would bring in. To my disappointment, it sold nothing. Zero. And it was exactly the same with my next four books. "Maybe this selling books on Amazon won't work after all?", I thought. Maybe it was just another online scam and I had fallen right into the trap.

But then, when I published my sixth book, something happened. The book started selling. It didn't sell much, just a few copies a week, but for me it was enough proof that this was working.

Now let's fast forward a few years. Since I published my first books in 2016, I've published *many more* books in several different niches and I've gradually built up a portfolio of books that generates a steady passive income every month. At the time of writing, my books have sold over 30,000 copies in total and generated over $100,000, which I am of course pleased with, but even so, I still feel like I'm only scratching the surface of what can actually be achieved by selling books on Amazon.

If you're reading this, you may be dreaming of building up an extra income online so you can cut down on working hours, afford to travel more, or want the opportunity to save and invest more money for the future. Publishing and selling books on Amazon is one way that can give you that passive extra income that makes it possible.

The benefits of selling books are many, and one of the main advantages of selling books is that the book as a product has been around since time immemorial. We humans have always read books and probably always will, which means that a book has the potential to generate revenue for many years to come. Another great thing about selling books on Amazon in particular is the amount of traffic that flows to the site. Over 80 million people visit Amazon every day!

This book contains everything you need to know to publish your own books on Amazon, both with the help of ghostwriters, or for those who prefer to write themselves. Everything I've learned about selling books on Amazon, from first browsing Project Life Mastery that summer evening, to all the courses, books and not least conversations with other Amazon publishers, along with my own tests and analysis is collected in the pages that follow.

My goal with this book is that by the time you finish reading, you will have learned how to produce, publish and market books on Amazon that can generate income for you every month. I hope that I succeed in delivering that to you.

1. Self-publishing on Amazon explodes as a passive income business

The book industry distinguishes between traditional publishing and self-publishing. Traditional publishing means that there is a book publisher involved. Self-publishing, on the other hand, means that the author publishes his or her book on his or her own, without the help of a publisher. Amazon launched its self-publishing service Kindle Direct Publishing (KDP) back in November 2007.

If I go back and try to find information about when self-publishing on Amazon as a passive income business started to be written about, it was not until the mid-2010s that the first blog posts addressed the topic at all. The person who was at the forefront then and who is also considered to be the one who made self-publishing on Amazon more mainstream was Stefan James of Project Life Mastery. What made people take notice of him in particular was that he attracted an audience that was basically more interested in making money than in publishing books.

Stefan's approach to self-publishing on Amazon was all about using the books as a tool to generate passive income. To achieve this, he outsourced as much as possible of the process of producing a book. He hired cheap ghostwriters to write the text, cheap designers to make the covers, and cheap assistants to market the books. In this way, he could publish many books at low cost in a very short time and he did not depend on a single book becoming a bestseller. Stefan's model was to build up a large portfolio of books that sold well enough to generate passive royalties, much like having a stock portfolio that generates passive income through stock dividends.

Before Stefan started openly writing about what he did, most people thought that you had to be a writer to write a book and that you needed a publisher to publish it. Stefan's strategy of outsourcing the production process of his books and then publishing them himself made more people aware of the possibilities of self-publishing on Amazon.

I can only imagine how the authors who may have struggled this year with their manuscripts must have felt when the market was suddenly flooded with books written by ghostwriters. Before 2007, authors had fought hard to get publishers to publish their books, and now that they could finally self-publish on Amazon, people (myself included) began flocking to Amazon to see if it was really possible to make a passive income from publishing ghostwritten books.

The reason it works so well to publish ghostwritten books on Amazon and have the books generate passive income is because of the way Amazon is structured. In David Gaughran's book *Amazon Decoded*, David lifts the Amazon hood and explains how the Amazon engine works and how all the parts fit together. I'll try to summarize it in broad strokes for you here, but I really recommend that you read *Amazon Decoded* if you want to dig in even deeper.

The war between Yahoo! and Google laid the groundwork for how Amazon works today

Amazon's founder, Jeff Bezos, was one of the first investors in Google in the early 2000s. At the time, Google was only in its start-up phase and the search engine market was dominated by the then giant Yahoo!. They discovered quite early that it was big business to let companies advertise their products and services when someone searched on their search engine. Nowadays we are used to seeing ads everywhere on the internet, but paid advertising in connection with information searches was something completely new in the early 2000s.

Yahoo! obviously wanted to make as much money as they could from their ads and launched an advertising model whereby whoever paid the most to be seen for a keyword search would have their ad displayed. If a company paid one dollar to appear in a search for "weight loss" and another company paid two dollars to appear in a search for the same word, the company that paid two dollars got its ad shown. And this was the case regardless of whether the ad was about "weight loss" or not. This advertising model led to a war among large companies trying to get their ads seen on as many keywords as they could. This in turn drove the price of advertising (and Yahoo's! short-term revenue) sky high, but at the same time pushed out companies with a smaller budget who then had no chance of advertising on Yahoo! because it was so expensive.

For those using Yahoo! as their search engine, the effect was that many of the ads that appeared were not about what the person was looking for at all. Presumably both one and two users eventually got tired of seeing lots of irrelevant ads in connection with their searches.

So, when Google launched its advertising program, they did the opposite of what Yahoo! did. Instead, Google's advertising model was to display the most *relevant* ad possible based on the search that was made. If a person searched for "weight loss", Google wanted to show ads that were actually related to "weight loss". So, the big difference with this relevance model was that a lower bid ad could be shown instead of a higher bid ad, as long as Google thought the searcher was more likely to click on the cheaper ad. Google's strategy was thus to build trust with its users and the companies that advertised there.

Jeff Bezos stood on the side-lines and watched the war between Yahoo! and Google at close quarters, and what he noticed was how Google's strategy of presenting the most relevant ad possible far outperformed Yahoo's short-term "highest bid wins" strategy.

So, when Jeff Bezos built Amazon, he put the relevance factor at the heart of the whole structure. He wanted the customer to always feel that Amazon was presenting a product that the customer really wanted. He worked hard to build trust between the customer and Amazon so that the customer would come back again and again to buy more and more products.

For those who want to start selling, or are already selling books on Amazon, this is a particularly important factor because it means that Amazon is interested in the right customer finding a book that they are most likely to want to buy and read, regardless of who the author is. Amazon stores huge amounts of data about all its users and the spider in this web is a multitude of algorithms that work day and night to recommend the right book to the right customer. These book recommendations are not only visible on Amazon's site, but also in the personalized book recommendation emails that Amazon sends out to its customers several times a week.

The recommendation engine, combined with the relevance focus and the upwards of 80 million daily visitors that Amazon has, is what means that if you want to publish your own books, you have a good chance of selling lots of books on Amazon, even if you're not an established author.

2. See yourself as an author*preneur*

Do you know how many unfinished books are gathering dust in aspiring writers' drawers at home, waiting for the author in question to feel motivated to continue writing? Ten thousand? A hundred thousand? Ten million unfinished books? I can't possibly know the exact number, but I'm sure it's far too many!

At the start of your book publishing career, it's easy to feel motivation bubbling up inside, and rightly so. Publishing your own books on Amazon is fun. Feeling enthusiastic and energized about it is a good thing. Personally, I always get a motivation boost when I start a new book project on Amazon. But I still want to flag that motivation can be dangerous. Relying on your motivation to be the source of your energy, for motivation to be the engine that realizes your book idea and gets things done, is a tried-and-true strategy that doesn't work in the long run.

The dangerous, or rather unreliable, thing about motivation is that it comes and goes as it pleases. One day it's there and everything feels easy and fun, but the next day it's gone and everything feels heavy and boring. That motivation can be the fuel that kicks off your book project is not in doubt, but that motivation will be there by your side every time you plan to work on your book project and propel you forward throughout the journey is not something you can rely on.

The difference between those who succeed well and those who don't succeed at all in making money from publishing and selling their own books on Amazon is largely unrelated to motivation. A success factor for those who do succeed tends to be that they are prepared for the fact that it is a lot of work and that there are several parts of the publishing chain that need to work in order for a book to start selling and generating revenue. In the moment, they may not always have the motivation to get started, but that doesn't matter for those who have their sights set on success with their books. A term that is often used in this context when talking about motivation and what it takes to succeed is *authorpreneur*. I think it's an apt expression as it paints a good picture of how selling books is actually a business. An authorpreneur looks at their books as products and is aware that it takes much more than a "good text" to make money from them.

My approach to motivation is largely influenced by authors such as Robert Greene, Steven Pressfield, Ryan Holiday and Mark Manson. They write a lot about the way forward being on the other side of an obstacle and that progress happens when we expose ourselves to some kind of resistance. In the same way that you have to expose your muscles to resistance in order for them to grow, we have to expose our brains to different types of resistance in order for us to become mentally stronger. A lot of that mental resistance is not comfortable to "push" against, especially on those days when motivation is low. But it's largely a must for moving forward.

A concrete example of when I have to deal with that resistance is my attempt to put together this chapter that you are reading right now. It's not that I'm super motivated to write today, but I also can't just put off writing until some sunny day in the future when I might feel motivated, because I can't know for sure that that day will come. The risk of putting off writing would be that the book might never have been finished and it would have ended up in the drawer and become just another book in a series of unfinished books.

The fact that there is some resistance and that it is not necessarily always easy to succeed in selling books on Amazon is exactly what makes it valuable. Imagine if it had been super easy to publish books and get them to sell. If the threshold for making money and generating passive income had been so low that anyone could have done it without the slightest resistance. What would have happened then? Everyone would have done it. And do you know what things that virtually anyone can do often have in common? It's not valued very highly in the marketplace and it's hard to make any money from it.

But just because I write that you shouldn't rely on your motivation and that it's good that it will be difficult at times, doesn't automatically make it easier for you to succeed, does it?! So how are you going to succeed? What you need is a system that you can rely on through thick and thin and that doesn't depend on your mood or your motivation. A system that can break down all the upcoming obstacles into small pieces and tackle them one by one, making sure you keep moving forward. A system that is like a compass that shows you the way, even if the visibility is poorer one day.

In all the years I've been publishing on Amazon, I've tried to develop and refine a system that allows me to constantly publish new books and grow my own book business, without it taking too much of my calendar or my mental energy. I call my system the *Publishing System* and it consists mainly of three parts; input, process and output.

Inputs are the resources available in terms of time, energy and money. *Process* is the actual allocation of resources to get the maximum effect out of them and *Output* is what input and process together produce, which is measured in *value to the market*, and ultimately is what will determine whether your books will sell or not.

Input

Most people who start self-publishing on Amazon do so alongside an already busy schedule of full-time work, family and leisure activities. The time and energy that can be devoted to a book project is then scarce, often perhaps only a few hours a week.

When it comes to input, a generally good mindset is to focus on getting the most out of the resources available. For example, if you have two hours a week to work on your book, try to make the most of those two hours instead of wishing there was more time. The same goes for finances. If you want to publish a book but have limited financial resources, then you can publish a shorter book (lower cost for ghostwriters), write the book yourself, or publish some kind of activity book (more on activity books in Chapter 14), to keep costs down.

How to make the most of what you have

Have you heard of *Parkinson's Law*? It says that a task takes as long as you give it. Let's say you give yourself two weeks to work on a book idea. According to Parkinson's Law, it will then take you two weeks to do it. However, if you only give yourself three days to work on a book idea, then you will solve it in three days.

To get the best out of the resources you have, I advocate a somewhat extreme approach to Parkinson's Law. The time you give yourself to go from zero to having the book available on Amazon's platform, ready to generate royalties, will be directly reflected in the energy with which you tackle your book project. This is especially important right at the start of your book project. Getting into the habit of regularly working on your book project once or several times a week is better than sprinting once a month. Sometimes that might mean all the time you have is 45 minutes a week. Then it's still better to make the most of those 45 minutes than not.

One strategy I use to make the most of the time I have is to plan ahead as much as possible what to do. These planning sessions are a separate activity and are carried out at a separate time, completely separate from when I am working. The planning is done in three levels; quarterly, weekly and a plan for each day. The quarterly plan is an overall strategic plan that broadly acts as a roadmap for everything I want to focus on for that given quarter. It includes everything from relationships, training, my regular full-time job and of course how I intend to grow my book business in the next quarter. For example, it might say that I'm going to "research new book ideas, test new marketing strategies on book X and Y, or work on developing and updating some of my existing books". The idea of the quarterly plan is not that it should list exact activities, but rather that it guides how I do my weekly planning.

Every week I make a weekly plan based on the quarterly plan. Usually, I do the weekly planning on Sunday evening or Monday morning. When planning for the coming week, I always look at the quarterly plan and try to figure out how to best use the time available in the coming week to achieve what is in the quarterly plan. This means looking at my work calendar and my personal calendar and trying to estimate how much time I have available in the coming week for different activities. Weekly planning is much more specific than quarterly planning. For example, if the quarterly plan says I'm going to "research new book ideas", I'll rewrite it to "spend an hour doing research in the New Age niche" in the weekly plan.

The weekly plan in turn determines how I plan my days. Every day, before I start work, I look at the calendar for that particular day and compare it to my weekly plan. Then I try to figure out how best to put together that day's activities, meetings and other things to do, so that I get as much out of the day as possible. This means that in the morning I plan what I want my work day to look like, when I will do what and how long I expect the different activities to take. This daily planning is not set in stone, depending on how the day unfolds I may have to replan once or twice. The idea of this daily plan is not that it should be kept at all costs, but that there should be an awareness of how I can best make the most of a working day and that I consciously confront the reality of how long things take.

The good thing about planning in three different levels is that all the thinking and strategic planning is done up front, then everything that comes after that is based on using the resources to the maximum to execute the strategic plan. It becomes like a chain where all activities have a clear link to a long-term goal.

Planning and being proactive is the key to getting the most out of your working days, as it eliminates the "well, what am I going to do now?" question. Also, when I plan in this way, I don't have to have an internal debate with myself about what to work on next as those decisions are already made higher up in the planning structure.

A common comment I get when I talk about planning in this way is that it takes a lot of time to plan and that time should be spent working instead. It is true that planning takes time, but planning is not really something that takes time away from work, but rather should be seen as an investment to make the most of the time available. Anyone who does not put time and energy into thinking and planning in advance risks ending up in a very reactive way of working, where what is always the most urgent is the one that gets all the attention. It is also easy to fall into the trap of "working hard" without the work actually going anywhere or having a link to your long-term goal.

Process

Imagine that you put a sheet of metal into one end of a machine and ten cans of metal come out the other end of the machine. What happens in between is defined as a process, so a process is what happens between input and output.

In business, there is a certain penchant for always chasing more. More money, more followers or more visitors to the website. In order to achieve "more", the only solution is usually to work "harder", i.e., to increase the amount of input. But I would say that this is another trap. If you, like me, have other interests in life than working all day, we don't have unlimited input. That's why I think it's interesting to think extra carefully about the process we use. If I use the example of the tin plate and the tin cans again, there are lots of different ways that one tin plate can be turned into ten tin cans. It is possible to put the sheet into a modern robot that solves everything in a flash, with the push of a button. But it's just as easy to make tin cans with an older machine that requires reloading and hand layering, just that it takes longer.

Similarly, there are several different processes you can use to go from zero to a finished book on Amazon. Common to all processes is that they contain a series of steps that turn input into output. In my opinion, a good process is one that has minimal waste between the different steps in the process. To illustrate the difference between a good and a less good process, imagine researching Amazon for potential book ideas. You browse around inside Amazon for inspiration and look at what other books are available. A good process would then involve gathering all your research into some kind of document that you can easily find your way back to so you don't have to do the same research job again later on. A good process would also involve pushing a piece of work to a natural break or end point and, before you finish for the day, gathering all your thoughts and reflections on the way forward to avoid unnecessary waste between work sessions. Contrast this with a less good process that might involve not gathering your research, not gathering your thoughts and reflections and not working to a natural break or end point. Such a less-than-good process easily results in duplication of effort and long start-up times between your work occasions.

The combination of having a clear planning structure that ensures the right tasks are done at the right time, together with a work process that eliminates waste, is the foundation of the Publishing System and, in my opinion, the foundation of success as a writer. Exactly what tasks you need to do to publish a book that generates royalties is what the remaining chapters of this book are about.

Output

If there's one thing that's often talked about in online business circles, it's creating value. You've probably read posts on social media where it's usually advised to create "valuable posts" and give your audience something of "value", but what does it really mean to create value?

It is not always clear what the word *value* means. A basic prerequisite for even being able to create value is to know your target group and what they *value*. What is valuable to someone is a subjective judgement, which means that two people can read exactly the same book and one may find the book valuable while the other finds it a complete waste of time.

Value is not a zero-sum game
Earlier in life, as you already know, one of my great interests was online poker. A prerequisite for me to have been able to win money playing poker is, by default, that someone must have lost money. In poker, there is only a predetermined amount of money in play for each deal. In other words, poker is something called a zero-sum game. After a poker hand has ended, there is no more or less than there was before, the money has just changed hands.

If you imagine that you have a zero-sum game on one side of a spectrum, then you can imagine that "value" lives on the other side of the same spectrum. In other words, when you talk about value, you mean things that are not a zero-sum game. Let's say you publish a book that makes your target audience's life better, then you've effectively created value. Value is created by filling a void where there was none before. It should also be said that if you deliberately publish a book that you know is bad, where you don't care about your target audience and where you just want their money to move to you, then according to this line of thinking you have not created any value.

Use the Publishing System to help you structure your book project
The input, process and output publishing system can help you structure how you move your book project forward without it taking up too much of your calendar or mental energy. Combine the

Publishing System with an authorpreneur mindset and you're all set for success now that it's time to start researching a book idea that you know Amazon's customers will want to pay for long before you publish the book.

3. Publish a book that you know Amazon customers will buy

One of my absolute favorite authors is Cal Newport. He writes nonfiction in a relatively narrow niche, focusing on career development and productivity. What I like about Cal's books is that he challenges recurring mainstream advice like "find your passion" and "write a to-do list." Cal is the author of many books, including the bestsellers *Deep Work*, *Digital Minimalism* and *A World Without E-mail*. He also runs the podcast *Deep Questions*, which basically involves him answering listeners' various questions. Every now and then, Cal answers book publishing-related questions like "how do I get a book published?" or "can you share some tips on why a publisher chooses to publish a particular book?". When these types of questions come up, I always turn up the volume to the max and listen intently to what he has to say. Cal is a true super-professional and he spares no expense in his expositions, which are also very useful for all of us who publish books on our own, without the help of a publisher.

According to Cal Newport, there are three criteria that must be met for a publisher to even consider publishing a book. While there are a lot of differences between publishing a book through a real publisher and self-publishing a book on Amazon, these criteria can still be useful to know. Please think about how you can apply the criteria to your book project.

Criterion one: There must be an audience willing to pay money for the book.

Imagine you own a book publishing company. What would be important to you then? Most likely, you would have had a vested interest in the books that the publisher published selling like hot cakes, because then the publisher - and you - would have made a lot of money. A book publisher's business is simply to publish books that people want to *buy*. Therefore, for a publisher to consider publishing a book, it must be written in such a way that it is aimed at a well-defined audience.

As a self-publisher, this means that the very basis of the book - *the book idea* - must be clear enough to find evidence that there is an audience willing to pay money for that kind of book. If there isn't an audience, then it will be difficult to get the book to sell.

Criterion two: the author must be a good enough writer.

To be published as a non-fiction author by a publisher, there is no requirement to be famous or to have won literary prizes. However, the quality of the text in the book must be sufficiently high so that the reader does not perceive the book as amateurishly written. The publisher ensures that the text, and the book in general, is of sufficiently high quality by involving a variety of professionals such as editors, designers and others in shaping the text and appearance of the book.

Since many of us who self-publish on Amazon do so as a way to make money, we don't necessarily have any interest in writing our own books. Instead, many of us are more than happy to hire ghostwriters for that job. Usually, outsourcing the writing to a ghostwriter is not a problem, as most ghostwriters write well enough that the reader does not perceive the text as amateurish. However, it is still important to proofread the text that the ghostwriter has written to ensure that it is of sufficient quality. Of course, if you are writing your own book, it is also important to have someone who can proofread and ensure the quality of the text.

Criterion three: the book must be written by the right person. The third and final criterion that Cal usually talks about is that the book should be written by the right person. This means that a publisher will not let just anyone write a book about just anything. The author needs to have experience in the subject matter of the book for the book to be credible. As an example, consider a person who wants to pitch a publisher with an idea for a vegan cookbook. Then, for example, the person should have experience eating a vegan diet and perhaps also be knowledgeable about vegan nutrition, to be the "right" person to write the book.

One of the advantages of hiring a ghostwriter and self-publishing a book is that you can easily parry this third criterion. In principle, you can publish a book on anything, even a subject you have no experience or knowledge of. In fact, it is possible to construct the image that you are the right person to publish the book by publishing your book under a fictitious author's name, a so-called pseudonym. Publishing a book under a pseudonym may seem fake, but it is not at all uncommon in the book industry and nothing to be afraid of. I myself have published the majority of my books under a pseudonym and sometimes I have even published them under a made-up girl's name in order to paint a better picture that the books are written by the right person and thus increase the credibility of the books.

Amazon as a bookstore

Amazon is the world's largest bookstore. On Amazon there are over ten million different books in over 13,000 different book categories. Planning a grand party? Then head to the party planning category and scroll through hundreds of party fixer books to get inspired and learn how to fold tailgating napkins that will make a big impression on all your guests. Want to teach your parrot to talk? Then head to the parrot category. Or would you rather read a classic thriller? Then click through to the classic thriller category. On Amazon, there are books on just about *everything*, and more.

One of the most common questions I get from people who are curious about starting their own books is usually about finding a good book idea. The question usually goes something like; *Do you have any ideas about what my book could be about? Preferably something that sells well, because I don't want to make a mistake and lose money!*

Going through the process of working out a book idea worth publishing is usually the first hurdle on the journey to monetizing Amazon publishing. Doing book idea research can feel hopeless for anyone who doesn't find a good book idea fast enough, but initially, in the startup of your first book projects, the goal isn't necessarily to find the perfect book idea. Instead, the goal is to find a book idea that is *good enough* that Amazon's customers will be interested in paying money to buy the book.

For me, it took several attempts before I managed to publish a book that Amazon's customers actually wanted to pay money for. My first five books totally flopped, largely because my book ideas weren't good enough. My hope is that with the help of this book, you will avoid making the same mistakes I did and not have to publish five books before you get your sales going. To find a good enough book idea, you can use my research process later in the chapter.

Writing to market for non-fiction

In self-publishing, there is an expression called *writing to market*. The term gained currency after Chris Fox published the book *Write to Market: Deliver a Book that Sells*. It is a book aimed primarily at fiction writers, helping them to develop a commercially attractive book idea in a genre that the market wants. Although Chris's book is aimed primarily at fiction writers, the very concept of writing to market is just as important in non-fiction. Cal Newport's second criterion I just wrote about, that there must be an audience for the book, is partly what writing to market is all about.

I know from experience that it can be tempting to turn a blind eye to writing to market and instead write and publish a book that has been on your mind for a while, for example a book about your "own journey", your childhood or about yourself. There's absolutely nothing wrong with that. The important thing is just to think about what your goal is with your book and adjust your expectations accordingly.

Commercial book ideas

The first step in developing your own book idea is to think briefly about why people pay money to buy and read non-fiction books in the first place. Is it for the entertainment value? Is it because the person in question is particularly interested in a subject? Is it as a pastime? There are, of course, many different reasons why someone reads non-fiction, but the vast majority of people who read non-fiction do so to get answers to a question of some kind. It is also not uncommon for the question the reader wants answered to be an urgent one. For the reader, that urgent question may be perceived as a problem in his or her life, where an answer to that urgent question would make life considerably better. When enough readers have the same acute question, a demand for a certain type of book arises. To deliver the answer to such a question in book form is simply to write to the market.

The idea of the research process that follows is to help you identify one or more pressing issues for Amazon's customers. Once you know what that issue or issues are, you can shape your book idea to include the answer to that particular question. The definition of writing to market, then, is: *finding a hungry audience with an urgent need to address a pressing problem/issue and offering them the solution in book form.*

To illustrate how writing to market works in practice, imagine two seemingly equivalent books where one is a bestseller and the other a flop. Why does one sell but not the other? There could, of course, be a number of different parameters at play. Usually, the answer to that question crystallizes when you study in detail the underlying book idea and structure of each book. If this is done, it usually becomes clear that the best-selling book often has writing to market built into its design and that everything about the book is based on it fitting into the market and solving an urgent issue for a hungry audience. So, it's clear what it *does* for the reader. On the contrary, a book that flops often has several flaws in its presentation and readers do not really understand what to expect from the book and therefore refrain from buying it.

Many of the things we struggle with today - relationships, health, money or child rearing - are things we struggled with even hundreds of years ago and will struggle with even hundreds of years from now.

These are issues that are deeply rooted in our human nature and that are ever as urgent and timely. What is typical of a writing-to-market book is that it focuses on precisely these pressing, often timeless, issues, and they often form the backbone of the book. After the pressing issues have been built into the book, the book is dressed up with examples and ideas that the reader can relate to.

A side effect of seeing a book as an answer to the reader's questions or as a solution to the reader's problems is that the book also automatically falls into a commercial niche. In such a niche there is a demand, which is a must if your book project is to generate income. A sign that you have found a commercial niche where demand is high is that there are many similar books that in some way shed light on the same underlying issue. The fact that similar books already exist is a good sign. Unlike many other products, a book is not a rare commodity. Most people who read books tend to read regularly and are constantly on the lookout for new books. Imagine a reader who is interested in earning more money and advancing in their career. How many career books do you think the reader will buy over a five-year period? Probably several. The fact that the book is not a rare purchase and that readers tend to buy new books all the time is important to highlight. So, hesitating to go ahead with a book idea just because there are other books about the same subject is not the right strategy.

Start working on a write-to-market book
So far, this book has been very theoretical. We've gone over how Amazon works, what you can do to get the most out of your resources, and what writing to market means, among other things. Now it's just about time to drop the theory for a while and get down to the more practical work.

Publishing a book on Amazon, as you know, requires a book idea worth developing into a real book, whether you hire a ghostwriter or write it yourself. To get started, my suggestion is to start brainstorming different book ideas. Brainstorming may seem like a bit of a simplistic approach, but the idea of brainstorming is that it should act as a gateway to different ideas that you can then explore further inside Amazon. While you're on Amazon exploring your book ideas, you'll see lots of other books and get new ideas. In a way, it's like a feedback loop where you gradually get more and more book ideas and hopefully also a better sense of the pressing issue you want to answer in your book.

Get started with brainstorming

List as many different book ideas as you can think of. You can brainstorm as broadly or narrowly as you like. There are no limits and no right or wrong. Some examples of book ideas could be; yoga for beginners, how to get rid of an addiction, dating for men 50+, workout tips for home exercise or social media marketing.

To help you brainstorm, think about what people around you tend to talk about as problems. Maybe they are stressed? Maybe they have a boring job that sucks all their energy? Are they tired of their screaming children? By trying to imagine yourself in situations where people around you express that they have a problem with something, you can shape their problem or issue into suitable book ideas. Another way to brainstorm is to focus on what you are good at. What are your top three qualifications according to your friends? Write them down on a piece of paper.

When you're brainstorming, it's easy to think "ugh, everyone knows that, I can't do a book about that", but remember that what's easy for you can be a big hassle for many others, so write down all the ideas you come up with!

Filter the book ideas through the write-to-market filter

Once you have your various book ideas in front of you, it's time to start crossing out the ones that are less good and keeping the ones that have the potential to become a book. To know which book ideas are good or not so good, let's run them through what I call the *write-to-market filter*. The filter consists of four questions, where each book idea must get a resounding "yes" to qualify for the next question. When passing your book ideas through the filter, try to be as objective as you can, and try to see them from the perspective of Amazon's customers.

1.   Do people even read books about [insert your book idea]?

If the answer to that question is no, you can put that book idea aside right away. An example might be that you had an idea for a book on how to inline skate, but when you think about it, you might realise that nobody reads books about inline skating. Most things in that category might be video related, in which case you might as well drop your inline skating book idea right away.

2.   Does your book idea solve a pressing issue?

Different issues have different urgency. The more pressing the issue your book highlights, the more potential it has to sell. You can get a sense of how urgent an issue is by imagining how likely it is that someone will wake up in the middle of the night and articulate the issue to themselves. For example, relatively few people are likely to be sleepless at night because of weeds in the driveway (a less acute problem), while many more are likely to be sleepless because they don't want to keep going to a job they hate (urgency to find a solution and alternative career paths). A book that solves an acute issue is much closer to writing for the market than a book that solves a non-acute issue.

3. Does your book idea highlight a timeless issue?

For your book to sell for years to come, it is important that it highlights a timeless issue. An example of a timeless question is "how do I find a love partner?". We humans have always had questions related to our relationships, so if you publish a relationship book, you are guaranteed to highlight a perennial question. If, on the other hand, you produce a book that is very much stuck in today's trends and packed with information about how things work today, for example a book about electric cars, you run the risk of the book becoming outdated as soon as something on the subject develops, or newer technology comes along.

4. Is it possible for a ghostwriter to write the book or does it require more in-depth research and knowledge?

If you want to write your book yourself, you don't have to worry about ghostwriters at all, and can then ignore this issue altogether. If, on the other hand, you want to publish books without writing them yourself, then the ghostwriter is a key person in your book project, provided that the ghostwriter can actually write a readable book. This is usually not a problem as long as the subject matter of the book is not too technically difficult or requires deep knowledge of detail. For those who want to use ghostwriters, my advice is to put a lot of effort into your book order (how to write a good book order you can read about in chapter 5) so that you give the ghostwriter the conditions to do a good job.

Start by researching demand

Take your list of all the book ideas that made it through the write-to-market filter and translate them into keywords/keyword phrases. The book idea "a book about investing" is translated into the keyword "investing". The book idea "a book about social media marketing" translates to the search phrase "social media marketing". The book idea "yoga book for seniors" is translated into "yoga for seniors", and so on.

Once you've translated all your book ideas into keywords/phrases, it's time to take them to Amazon and see what the demand is like there. I recommend doing your research on the US Amazon, i.e., Amazon.com if you intend to publish English books. It is likely that the majority of your future revenue will come from sales in the US, which is why it is best to do the research there. If you do your research on another country's Amazon site (e.g., Amazon.ca), there is a risk that you will get a misleading picture of the actual demand, as each country's Amazon site is independent of the others and demand in the different countries differs somewhat.

Visit Amazon.com. At the top of the page, you will see a large search box. There you select that you want to search the "Kindle Store", type in your keyword/search phrase and press enter. If you have done this correctly, your search will result in a feed of books related to your keyword/search phrase. If you look at the top left of the image, you will see that it says "1-16 of over X results for", where X varies according to the keyword/phrase you have entered. The number of hits you get, i.e., the number on your "X" is what I will refer to as the *market* from now on. In other words, the market is the number of hits you get when you search for a particular keyword or search phrase.

I was going to include a picture here to visualize how this search works and what it looks like, but it was small and not clear enough. Instead, I have posted all the pictures on my website inkomstmedbocker.se/extra. Feel free to surf in and look there if you want a step-by-step guide on how to search on Amazon to see how big the market is for the search phrase "social media marketing". "Social media marketing" is the search phrase I will be using most frequently as an example in this book in the future.

Researching the size of the market is just one part of finding a book idea that you can develop into a book that Amazon's customers will want to pay money for. The reason why I recommend that you research the market size of all your book ideas is partly because I don't want you to publish a book that no one wants, and partly because I don't want you to publish a book in a market that's too big, where the competition is too high.

If I search for "social media marketing", at the time of writing, it returns about 10,000 hits in the US Kindle Store. The question then is, are 10,000 hits many or few and what does that number really mean?

If the search phrase "social media marketing" returns 10,000 hits, this means that Amazon selects from all the millions of books published on Amazon and then presents all the books that it believes are relevant to the search phrase "social media marketing", which is 10,000 books. Remember that Amazon is built around relevance, which means that if I, as an Amazon customer, search for "social media marketing" in the Kindle Store, only books that are about that particular topic are presented in the feed.

As a reference to the 10,000 number of books that showed up when I searched for "social media marketing", there are millions of different books in the Kindle Store. If we put 10,000 in relation to several million, 10,000 is not very much. But the truth is that of the 10,000 books displayed for the keyword "social media marketing", only a few hundred of them actually sell and even fewer of them sell reasonably well.

When you're new to Amazon publishing and working on your first book project, my recommendation is to use the size of the market as a guideline for which book ideas to work on. Look for a market where you get between 500 - 10,000 hits. Within that range, there is a good balance between the market being large enough to make money, but not so large that the competition is overwhelming.

If you are struggling to find a market with between 500 - 10,000 hits, try making your keywords/search phrases narrower and more specific. An example could be to specify the keyword "social media marketing" to "Instagram marketing for beginners" which results in a market of 520 hits at the time of writing.

One tip is to limit the keyword/search phrase to a maximum of five words. The keyword/search phrase should reflect what a potential Amazon customer might type into the search box to find a book, which is usually just somewhere between one to five words. Another reason not to have too many words in your search phrase is because the search phrase will advantageously appear, at least in whole or in part, in the title of the book later on. You then want to be able to have as "clean" a book title as possible, but more on that later.

Experiment with different keywords/phrases until you have five book ideas that fall within the range of 500 - 10,000 hits. If you can't do that, here's a little trick. Say you keep getting 20,000 hits whatever you search for, then you can check out the first books for each search and scan those books' reviews for other keyword clues. At one point when I was coaching a person, we were doing research in the dating niche but were having trouble finding a really good entry point. It wasn't until we read the reviews that we found further and realized that many readers complained that the dating books were not suitable for girls with children, which many of the readers cited as a preference. This opened up a new niche in "single mom dating" that we might otherwise never have thought of ourselves.

Find out if Amazon customers buy books similar to your book ideas

Once you have your five book ideas with a couple of keywords/search phrases in the 500 - 10,000 range, it's time to examine the extent to which Amazon's customers buy those types of books. Having customers actually buy the books is the foundation to making money from publishing books on Amazon.

To examine how well (or not so well) similar books to your book idea are selling, you need to examine Amazon's *best seller rank*. Start by re-entering your keyword/search phrase in the search box. When searching, it is important that you have selected that you are searching the Kindle Store and not just Amazon at large, as the *Kindle Store* will cause the search to be limited to showing only e-books. If you search on Amazon at large, you will get other types of products in the search results, and you don't want that. Aim for the first five or six books that show up in the feed, assuming they are similar to your book idea. If they don't resemble your book idea, keep scrolling the feed until you find a total of five or six books that do.

Click on the books that are similar to your book idea, one at a time, and scroll down to "product details" at the bottom of the book's product page. There is something called "best seller rank", sometimes called BSR. This ranking is a snapshot of how well the book you're looking at is currently selling compared to all the other e-books on Amazon. For example, if the book has a ranking of #37,899 that means there are 37,898 books selling better than that book right now. What happens when a customer buys a book on Amazon is that the ranking goes down and the book moves closer to #1. So a book with a low ranking sells better than a book with a high ranking.

All books in the Kindle Store have a ranking, provided the book has sold at least one copy. An indication that a book has recently sold a copy is that it is ranked #100,000 or lower. In this step, you want to identify a keyword/search phrase with as few search results in the 500 - 10,000 range as possible, while the first five to six books in the stream are ranked as low as possible. Such a keyword is ideal because you have evidence that several books in that market are actually selling, while the competition from other books is manageable.

Start from your own list of keywords/search phrases and analyse the market. If the first five or six books in the stream for your keyword/phrase have an amazon best seller rank of #100,000 or lower, you have found a potentially good keyword/phrase to move forward with. This means that the book idea is good enough to be worth developing into a real book.

Another way to examine the best seller rank of similar books is to analyze how well the books in a particular category sell. Again, if you click on a book similar to your book idea, scroll down to "product details" a bit down the book's product page, you will see that it says that the book also has different rankings in different categories. Next to the ranking you can click on a specific category. If I search for "social media marketing" and click on one of the first five books that come up in the feed and scroll down until I see the category ranking, one of the categories I see is "E-commerce (Kindle Store)". Clicking on that category takes me to the top 100 list of all books included in the "E-commerce" category in the Kindle Store. Once in the top 100 list, I can analyze the best seller rank for all the best-selling books in that category. If I then see that the top ranked books in that category have a best seller rank of less than #100,000, I can be sure that Amazon's customers are buying books related to "E-commerce".

If this demand analysis seems difficult, go to inkomstmedbocker.se/extra and check out the pictures I've posted. Hopefully it will be easier then.

4. How to develop your book idea into a book that Amazon customers want to pay money for

When aspiring writers come to marketing guru and author Seth Godin for some sympathy because their writing is so bad it's barely fit for toilet paper, Seth usually smiles and asks "Can you show me your bad work?". The strange thing is that once Seth has asked to see their writing, the aspiring writers rarely have anything to show. All half-finished books and incoherent articles disappear without a trace.

The fact that you have brainstormed and written down your own book ideas is great. It means there's something concrete to work on, so you can move forward in the process and get closer to your goal of publishing that bestseller. But if you only have an idea of what ideas you might, possibly one day, develop into an actual book, it's unfortunately not enough. The way forward is to start working on the book idea(s) that you can take on and keep working on developing them into actual books. If you're stuck in the research stage and haven't found a book idea that you think is worth developing into an actual book, I'm here to help. I say like Seth Godin, show me your bad book ideas! Email me at christian@inkomstmedbocker.se with the heading "My Book Ideas" and write down what book ideas you've brainstormed and where you've gotten stuck and I promise to help you.

Anyway, now it's time to move on. Dressing up your book idea with content and developing it into a real book doesn't have to be difficult.

The trick is to anchor the book's content in what readers want, answer their questions and make sure the book makes their lives better in some way. You probably remember the concept of writing to market. Now it's high time to turn that concept into a reality and once again shine the spotlight on *finding a hungry audience with an urgent need to address a pressing problem/issue and offer them the solution in book form.*

As I said, the book idea throughout this book is to publish a book on social media marketing. For the sake of simplicity, let's play with the idea that you are also thinking of publishing such a book and that it is now time to develop the book idea and dress the book with content. So how do you make sure the book answers your readers' questions and makes their lives better?

One way is to guess what the readers want. This can work, but the risk of guessing wrong and wasting time, money and energy developing a book that nobody wants to read is too great. A better way is to do research. In my opinion, research is a must even if you already feel you have a decent idea of what readers want.

How to research what the book should contain

Research is most easily done in two steps. Step one is to find out what the readers' urgent question is. You can then use that as the core of the book. Step two is to fill the book with content that delivers the answer to that question. Another way to formulate this is to first find out *what* problem the readers have, and then fill the book with information about *how* the readers solve the problem.

Research step 1. Find the most pressing issues of the book's target audience

When you start doing research, you may not know anyone in the book's ideal audience who you can pepper with questions to help you identify the most pressing issues for your target audience. But luckily, you don't have to. All the research you need to do to publish a good enough book is available in the open on Amazon and on various social media sites.

Research in Amazon reviews

Reading what Amazon's customers think about different books by reading and analyzing reviews is a real goldmine. Whenever I start a new book project and am in full swing of doing research, I always start from Amazon reviews. The reviews contain more or less all the information needed to find the most pressing issues of the book's target audience. My recommendation is that you spend the majority of your research time reviewing and analyzing Amazon reviews.

Before you start reading and analyzing reviews, I want you to put yourself in the perspective of Amazon's customers and think about what pressing issues those who bought a particular book might have had. To help you, consider the following issues when analyzing reviews:

- What pressing issue(s) did readers want answers to when they bought this book?
- In what ways did (or did not) the book succeed in delivering that?
- What concrete insights about the readers can I bring to my book project?

The idea of review research is to find new angles, insights and clues about the readers so that you can accurately identify the most pressing issues. To do this, you need to keep an open mind and try to be as objective as you can when doing your research. There is no prestige here; all research is done unbiasedly and you will have to practice keeping several, sometimes contradictory, insights in your head at the same time.

Furthermore, well-conducted research is also about stripping away all the layers of protective mechanisms and default responses of the readers as "everything is fine" and instead getting to the depth of what is going on inside them. You want to address emotionally charged issues where readers have an urgent need to find the answer to their question. You can think of research as a bit like walking on a minefield, where instead of avoiding the mines, you want to find them and step on them. When you step on an emotional mine, there will be an explosion of insights. That's where the gold and the target audience's most pressing issues are.

Of course, it's hard to get that kind of insight just by reading reviews on Amazon, as most reviewers don't tend to write any directly emotional long-winded posts. For example, a review along the lines of "great book" gives you nothing of value. What you need to do is look for reviews (number of stars doesn't matter) where the reader has put some effort into actually articulating themselves in an insightful way. When you read an insightful review, you will immediately feel that it resonates with authenticity and you will get a sense that you know what the reader wanted to get out of reading the book.

Just a finger of caution, before you get started. There are lots of fake reviews on Amazon. A fake review is a review that has been submitted in order to manipulate the perception of a book. For example, some Amazon publishers (who think they're smart) hire assistants from Bangladesh whose job it is to open fake Amazon accounts and post inflated fake reviews of their books day in and day out. Amazon is constantly working to clean up among these, but some always creep through, so pay attention.

One way to navigate past fake reviews and not be fooled by them is to turn up your bullshit detector to full power. If a review feels obviously fake, which is often characterized by barely describing the content of the book, being written with generic laudatory adjectives, and being published shortly after the book was released, it's probably fake.

Example analysis of two Amazon reviews
When it's time to do your review analysis, do this. Go to Amazon, click through to the Kindle store and search for your keyword/phrase. Choose one of the books that comes up high in the search feed that is similar to a book you would consider publishing. Click through to the book's product page and scroll down until you see all the reviews and start reading. Sometimes you need to read about twenty reviews before you get to a review that gives you the insights you need. To help you get into the mindset, we will now analyze together two different reviews that I have downloaded from Amazon.

Analysis of review one
Here's an authentic 3-star review from a book that comes up high in the search result for the keyword *social media marketing*. The review in

its entirety can be read at inkomstmedbocker.se/extra but I have cut the review text in italics here.

What I liked about the book:
- most social media engines covered
- some ok info on best practices

What I disliked:
- the book is rather lengthy, lots of fluff
- very little info on best practices, no case studies, no personal stories from the author
- the book is too technical ("go to the left corner and press publish" etc), even though you could probably figure most of that stuff yourself
- no pictures at all (probably because it would make this book much shorter)

So all in all, it's a good book if you can't figure yourself how to start a facebook ads campaign. But if you are looking for some new ideas from a seasoned veteran of marketing business, look elsewhere."

Now, when I do the review analysis, I try to put myself in the reader's perspective and think about what questions the reader who wrote the review must have had. Take a few minutes to think about what insights you get from reading the review before you read my analysis.

I can tell right away that the reader in question appreciated that it was a general book about social media marketing. But when I see such a statement, I never take it at face value, but I ask a counter question along the lines of "okay, do most people think a general book on social media marketing is better or would readers rather have platform-specific books?"

Furthermore, the reader writes that it was "ok info on best practices" while he writes "very little info on best practices, no case studies, no personal stories from the author" which makes me wonder what he really means. I don't need to come up with a definitive answer to that question at this point, but I just note what I see, take notes and ask myself open-ended counter-questions. One wonder I have is what he really means by "best practices".

To me, "best practices" sounds like a generic term that doesn't really say much. It makes me wonder if the reader himself knows what "best practices" are or if the reader just felt that the book tried to explain in an unclear way how the reader should go about succeeding in social media marketing. Another feeling I get when reading the review is that the reader perceives this book as a manual with too many technical aspects. I can imagine that by "too technical" the reader means that the book describes partly superfluous information about how to open accounts on different social media platforms and the like. The reader also points out that the book is far too long.

If I try to read between the lines and put myself in the reader's perspective, there are a couple of specific questions that come up, which I can deduce with a fair degree of certainty that the reader had hoped the book would answer. These are;

1. How do I make my social media marketing successful?
2. How have others done to succeed with social media marketing? Can I see proof that it works?
3. Can I get inspiration, tools and ideas for marketing campaigns that are more advanced in nature?

Although these are three concrete questions, I think they are a little too vague. The purpose of the review analysis is to boil down the review into a few specific questions combined with some notes and other insights that may be useful when you are working on finding relevant content for your book.

For example, the question "how do I succeed on social media?" is far too general. It needs to be more clearly identified what "succeeding on social media" means. A spontaneous feeling I have is that success equals getting customers and making money through social media. If I were to boil this review down into one concrete urgent question, it would be "how do I make money on social media?".

Analysis of review two

This is part of another authentic review on a book that came up high in the search result for the keyword "social media marketing". The book is about Instagram marketing. The review in its entirety can also be read on the website inkomstmedbocker.se/extra.

The bulk of this self-published book is comprised of basic tips you'll find for free anywhere online. Things like, post consistently, post attractive photos, engage with your followers blah blah blah. The only "secrets" were to PURCHASE shout-outs from huge accounts, which rarely applies to most folks. Or join shady groups where people all agree to go and like/follow each other. Who published this garbage? I'm mad that I bought it, but, this author appears good at getting people to hand him their money. Bad taste in my mouth. Do some research on this author and decide for yourself.

Put on your analytical glasses and think about what this reader is writing. What do you conclude? Think for a few minutes before reading my analysis.

The first thing I notice is that the reader seems upset that the book contains questionable strategies for growing your account on Instagram. The second thing I notice is that the reader had expected more from the book than what is already available to read for free online. This is important insight because it clarifies the reader's expectations of the book. For example, if you are doing a book on social media marketing, then you might ask yourself if the content of the book is such that anyone can find the exact same content on Wikipedia. If so, then you know that the book's content is not good enough and you will have to work harder to craft a message that is of higher quality and better answers the readers' questions.

When I read this review, I also get the feeling that the reader is very frustrated and feels cheated as the book has not nearly lived up to his expectations. The reader was probably hoping that the book would deliver many more strategies that "not everyone already knows", while he was also hoping for tips, where there should be no doubt about whether the strategies presented are allowed or not.

If I try to find the reader's actual question between the lines of this review, it could read something like; how do I grow on Instagram without using questionable/forbidden strategies?

The aim of the review analysis
Before we move on in the research process and develop the book idea further, I just want to flag that the issues I have identified in analysis one and two are of different urgency and broadly speaking I have only been able to conclude that readers find the information in the books far too superficial. These are good instincts in themselves, but I would have needed to do much more extensive review research before I could know with certainty that I had a comprehensive

picture of the most pressing issues of the target audience. My recommendation is to do review analysis on at least twenty different books to get a more comprehensive picture of what readers want.

The goal of the review analysis is to find Amazon's most pressing customer issues for your particular book idea. My recommendation to do review analysis on at least twenty books, is of course only an approximate number. You may need to analyze many more reviews than that. One way to know that you're getting close to finishing your review analysis is if you keep identifying the same pressing issues. Say you are analyzing five different authentic reviews each of three different books and you have identified two really pressing issues. The more reviews you analyze, the clearer it becomes that all readers have the same issues. Then you can be sure that you have found the core issues and you can feel done with the review analysis.

If, on the other hand, you have analyzed twenty reviews and identified a number of different pressing issues and feel that the more reviews you analyze, the more pressing issues you find, what do you do? Well, then you keep analyzing until you find no new pressing issues. When you start to finish the review analysis and find no new pressing issues, you can feel confident that you have a comprehensive picture of what Amazon's customers want answers to when they buy these types of books.

Research in social media and online forums
In addition to just analyzing on Amazon, you can also do research on social media and online forums. Which social media platforms and online forums you research is up to you. The most important thing is to find relevant sources such as niche Facebook groups, niche online forums or "influencers" that have an audience in the same

target group as your book idea. For example, if your book idea is about yoga for beginners, you can look for yoga forums, join a FB group dedicated to yoga or start following a yoga influencer.

The strategy for obtaining any research of value on social media and online forums is the same as for the review analysis on Amazon. So it's not about validating or confirming what you already know, but rather the opposite, being open to new insights and recurring questions. All in order to get as good and comprehensive a picture of readers' needs and wishes as possible.

Once you have done enough research to clearly identify the most pressing issues of your target audience, I think one of the most fun parts of the whole book project begins. Namely, piecing together and structuring all the insights into the body of your book! I'll explain how to do that in the next chapter.

5. Fine-tune the structure of the book before hiring a ghostwriter, or writing it yourself

For your book to deliver what the reader expects, the message in the book needs to be clear and follow a common thread. If it doesn't, the book can be perceived as scattered and the reading experience can be negatively affected. Let's turn our attention again to a book idea in the niche of "social media marketing" where we assume that I have identified the most pressing issue as *how do I best use social media to get more customers, sell more and make more money?*

As a common thread throughout the book, I will use this most pressing issue that I have now identified. This means that everything the book will contain, in one way or another, aims to provide the reader with answers to this question. The main purpose of the book - what the book does for the reader - then becomes crystal clear.

In order to fill the book with content, I also return to the other issues identified during the review analysis. An example of such could then be; *How have others done to achieve [include reader's desired outcome] through social media marketing? Can I see evidence that it works?* By rephrasing that question from the common thread perspective, I can fill in the reader's desired outcome and rephrase the question as *How have others done to gain customers through social media marketing? Can I see evidence that it works?*

When I feel confident that Amazon's customers are buying books on social media marketing to see how others have done to get customers through social media marketing and also want to see evidence that it works, then the opportunity to answer that question opens up in a variety of ways. For example, I could look up and compile different types of marketing campaigns that generated customers and sales and contrast them with campaigns that only generated likes, for example, and thereby draw different conclusions that can help the reader construct a successful marketing campaign. When I know what I want the book to do for the reader, that is, what the acute question is that is the backbone of the book, then I can answer it in an infinite number of ways.

Storytelling and the hero's journey

The purpose of publishing a non-fiction book is, as I have said so many times now, to give the reader answers to his most pressing question(s). But a book that contains only facts can easily be perceived as "boring" and uninspiring to read. To get around this and make the book more entertaining and readable, you can work storytelling into the book.

Superstar Will Smith's biography, the book *Will*, takes us on a journey as Will breaks into Hollywood as the highest paid actor. Will lines up blockbuster after blockbuster, and the way he does it is systematic and calculated. He writes in the book that he managed to crack the code of what it takes for a film to become a mega-success. In addition to cool effects and humorous lines, the film needs to follow a clear storytelling structure. The structure Will writes about is the timeless "hero's journey".

The hero's journey is by no means unique to Hollywood movies, it can be found in plays, fiction books and TV series, and can even be built into your next non-fiction book. The way I usually build the hero's journey into non-fiction books is borrowed from Steven Pressfield's brilliant book *Nobody Wants to Read Your Sh*t*. In it, Steven shares a framework that helps capture all the elements of the hero's journey. This framework is not the same as a table of contents, but should be seen as a guide to help you get started filling your book with content. Here are the six parts of Steven's framework.

One theme: what the book is about. What does the reader get out of the book? Here you fill in the common thread you want to have in your book.

A concept: what unique angle of [your book idea] does your book have compared to all other similar books? For example, in my case, with social media marketing, there are thousands of books on the market, so I need to think about why someone would want to read my particular book on the subject.

A hero: In non-fiction, a hero may seem remote, but the hero here is not an imaginary character as in fiction, but rather the hero in this type of book is usually the *reader* himself. You can imagine that the reader has a problem that needs to be solved, in order to get there, the reader has to complete a journey, the reader is then the hero of his or her own journey.

An enemy: The enemy in a non-fiction book is not a villain like in a James Bond movie, but the enemy is the obstacle that the reader (hero) is trying to get past. In a book about exercise, the enemy might be the reluctance to exercise, the lure of eating bad food, or the difficulty of breaking old habits.

An "all is lost" moment: every story has a moment where the hero is at rock bottom. A non-fiction book should also have such a moment. It's not always easy to pinpoint what should constitute an "all is lost" moment in the book. What you can do then is to consider whether you can build an "inciting incident" into the book instead.

An inciting incident is often used in fiction to set the story in motion and make clear the journey the hero is on. As an example, I wrote in the introduction to this book that the reason I started Amazon publishing was because I was tired of playing poker. That summer evening I write about at the beginning of the book is an inciting incident that sets this book in motion.

Climax: The moment when things turn around for the hero. It could be that the scales start to fall after weeks of hard work at the gym, that the hero finally gets a first date after years of loneliness or that the hero gets his first client for his business.

When I use Steven Pressfield's storytelling framework, I usually start with the questions I want my book to answer and then think about where they fit best. Let's say one of the questions I want to answer in the book is; *How do I (as in the reader) easily post social media posts that draw traffic to my website?*

Such a question can fit in several different places in Steven's framework, depending on what I want to get out of it and how I want it to relate to the common thread of the book. The hero in this case is the reader and the enemy is the difficulty of getting people to visit the hero's website. I could place the issue under "climax" and gradually tell stories and give examples of a number of "failures" before shifting focus and showing examples of strategies that actually work for using social media to drive traffic to a website.

So, the idea of this is to fill in Steven's framework based on the issues and the common thread of your book and make sure that the hero's journey is built into the book. In this way, the book will automatically be entertaining and inspiring for the reader, as the book contains several elements that the reader can relate to. This in turn sets the stage for the book to hopefully sell well for a long time.

Make a table of contents

If you list all the questions you want the book to answer and portion them out in the storytelling framework, you have more or less all the elements of your book ready in front of you. You'll see that the book will have a clear purpose with a common thread running through all the parts, all rooted in the very things that Amazon's customers want to pay money to read about. The only thing left to do before it's time to write the book is "just" to make a table of contents. The difference between Steven's story framework and a table of contents is that a table of contents is clearly divided into chapters, with each chapter spelling out what it will cover. For example, you may want to start your book with an "all is lost" section and gradually explain the book's concept before the book begins to answer the reader's questions.

I think making a table of contents is a must whether you write the book yourself or outsource the writing to a ghostwriter. The table of contents gives you a good overview of the book's contents and you can more easily see if you need to add or remove things even before you send off an order to the ghostwriter. For those who want to write themselves, you can use the table of contents as a planning tool, as you can clearly see which parts need to be written and how far along you are.

When I make a table of contents, I usually make a bulleted list and sometimes a short summary of what I want to convey in each chapter. This way, the table of contents gives an overview of the content of the book and I can get a good sense of whether the book will deliver what I hope it will. In the table of contents, I usually also include the way I want to convey it, with the three most common ways being through personal experience, historical examples or using research.

Personal experiences

An example of a book that is largely based on personal experience is this book you are reading now. It is written from my accumulated knowledge of publishing books on Amazon. I have tried to structure the book so that you, the reader, can be the hero on your own journey to get started making money on Amazon. An alternative to drawing on my experiences could have been to tell you how others have gone about making money from Amazon publishing. I'm sure that would have made a worthwhile book too, but I think in this case it's more impactful to talk about my own experiences. If you have personal experiences (that are relevant to your book), you could usefully build them in somewhere in the book, as at least a couple of personal examples are usually appreciated by readers!

Historical examples

Another way to present facts and illustrate the answer to a question is to give interesting examples of how others have done it. In the example of a book on social media marketing, let's say you want to show how readers can make their message go viral, but you don't have any experience with viral campaigns yourself. So how do you go about it? For example, in such a case, you could write about and analyze why the song Gangnam Style (remember it?) managed to break through and get people around the world to do the gallop dance and then draw parallels to how the same strategies could have been applied to social media marketing.

One advantage of using historical examples in the book is that there is endless inspiration and it is possible to illustrate the answer to readers' questions in many different ways and from many different angles, just by giving examples of how others have done it.

Research

Depending on the topic of your book, you can also include research reports that prove or disprove what the book argues. For example, if your book is about the impact of mobile phones on young people's concentration, you could include research on how much time young people spend on their phones each day and what this leads to. Just make sure that the research you refer to is reliable and that you always include the source.

Example of a table of contents

As an example of what Steven's storytelling framework combined with an overall table of contents looks like, I've cut and pasted a portion of it that I developed myself before I started writing this book. Here's what it looks like.

Storytelling

- Theme: Freedom? Make money on the side.
- Concept: using books as digital assets.
- Climax: First sales, proof that it works.

- Hero: the reader.
- Enemy: 9-5 job, status quo.
- Start: Inciting incident "I need to find something else" (tired of gambling, recognition).

Intro

- Inciting incident:
  Tell the reader about myself, my poker background, what the poker background can give you as clues how I got into self-publishing and why self-publishing is such a great way to make money.
- Connect to the reader that this book will contain everything needed.
- Tell them about the purpose of the book, and that this is like a guide, to succeed you have to do the work yourself.

Chapter 1

- Describe how self-publishing exploded as a side income.
- Google vs Yahoo!.
- Describe why selling on Amazon is a "big deal" (traffic, recommendations).

As you can see, the storytelling framework or the bulleted list of content is not polished in any way, but that's not the point here. What is important is that it gives a good overall picture of the storytelling I want in the book and what each chapter should be about. As the book came together, I added some elements and removed others, but by and large the original table of contents is the same and has also served as a planning tool throughout the writing process.

Turn the table of contents into an order for the ghostwriter

For those who think this ghostwriter thing sounds great and want to outsource the writing, you can use the storytelling framework and table of contents as the basis for commissioning the ghostwriter. What you need to add is a short summary of each chapter, the target audience of the book, make it clear what the book will do for the reader, the tone you want the book to be written in and how long the book should be. Once you've done that, you have everything you need to hire a ghostwriter!

Find the right ghostwriter

There are different ways to hire a ghostwriter. One way is to hire a freelance writer from an online freelance site such as Upwork or Fiverr. Another way is to hire a writing company. There are a few differences between a freelancer and a writing company, and there are pros and cons to both. The advantage of hiring a freelancer is that you usually have good visibility into the writing process and you can usually provide feedback on the text as it develops. If you hire a writing company, that option is usually not available. Instead, you provide feedback after the book is finished. This may mean that the writing company needs to make extensive rewrites or that there is an argument about whether or not they followed your order.

But there are benefits to hiring a writing company too. One of them is that a writing company has several different writers and professions within the company, which means that you as the client can feel confident that your book will be finished on time. If you commission the text from a freelancer and they fall ill, then your entire book project could be delayed. Another advantage of writing companies is that they usually guarantee that the text you buy is 100% unique. It may seem obvious that the text you buy should not be plagiarised, but unfortunately freelance writers sometimes plagiarise large parts of other books, or even entire books, just changing the names of certain chapters. If you happen to publish a plagiarized text, Amazon may suspend your account and take other action in the worst case, so make sure you get a guarantee that the text you buy is unique.

If you're hiring a ghostwriter for the first time, my recommendation is still to choose a writing company, as it gives you greater security as a client. There are lots of different writing companies, one of which I use and recommend is The Writing Summit (thewritingsummit.com). They have different prices depending on the type of writer you want to hire, but I definitely recommend ordering their best package, with English-native writers and editing included. The cost of that, at the time of this writing, is $3 per 100 words. I also have an affiliate partnership with The Writing Summit, which means you can get a 5% discount on orders with the code IMB5.

A book manuscript delivered by a ghostwriter is usually proof read, edited and ready for publication. However, I strongly recommend that you read the book carefully to make sure it is actually about what you intended. At one point, I published a couple of ghostwritten programming books without proof reading them and without knowing a thing about programming. It turned out afterwards that the ghostwriter didn't know a thing about programming either, but it wasn't until the 1-star reviews started pouring in that I realized it. After all, it's rare for a ghostwriter to take on writing the book without any prior knowledge, but it can happen and it's a risk that must be factored in. So be sure to read the book before publishing it.

How long should the book be?

Whether you write yourself or hire a ghostwriter, the book must answer the reader's questions and be well enough written not to be perceived as amateurish. The reader must get value for the time and energy it takes to read the book. The reader should of course get value for money too, but given that books are relatively cheap compared to other products, the reader's investment of time and energy is, in my opinion, more important.

How long a book needs to be to deliver that depends. There's no hard and fast rule, but there are a few guidelines to keep in mind. The length of a book is usually measured in word count and having the book be at least 10,000 words may be a minimum measure to stick to. This corresponds to about one hour of reading time, which in fact can often be enough for the reader to have a good reading experience and to have time to find the answers to their questions.

Some thoughts on writer's block for those who want to write for themselves

If you bought this book as a guide to getting your writing career off the ground on Amazon, and you have no plans whatsoever to use ghostwriters, then the whole ghostwriter thing may be more or less uninteresting to you. But then you're faced with another challenge, namely writing the book yourself and, in many cases, dealing with the writer's block that often entails.

Writer's block is a "state" where the writer sits staring at a blank piece of paper in front of them, waiting for the flash of inspiration to strike. Once the inspiration strikes, it is expected to transfer its magical power to the writer's fingers, which suddenly get a flow and start dancing across the keyboard. The dance results in the author producing fantastically composed sentences that can almost sing themselves, and all this happens, of course, without any effort on the part of the author.

The description above is a romanticized picture of the writing process. The tricky thing about writing is that sometimes you get that magical flow where inspiration flows and the words just pour out of you, but that flow stage is not a common occurrence. On the contrary, the writing process, at least for me, tends to require patience, determination and careful planning. By planning, I mean that I've thought through what I'm going to write before I write. This means that at the actual moment of writing, I never really start from a blank piece of paper, but I always have a plan for what I am going to write about that particular day.

Then I think that the thing with writer's block is often over-dramatized. Author Cal Newport, who I've written about before in this book, says that "what amateur writers call writer's block, professional writers call writing", which makes it clear that everyone, even the very best writers, can feel a resistance to putting words on paper at times. Another quote about writer's block comes from author Ryan Holiday, who says that "you can always edit a bad piece of writing, but you can never edit a piece of writing that doesn't exist".

Not making the writing process more difficult than it really is, I believe, is a recipe for success that will make writing easier for you as you write your own book. Instead of sitting around waiting for inspiration to strike, you can see writing as a process, where one way to get around the writer's block is to see your book's table of contents as a guide to what you should write. Let's say you've structured your book into 10 chapters, with each chapter being 2,500 words and starting with a personal story and ending with a brief summary of various research papers. Then you simply start writing on Chapter 1, Part 1, then you take Chapter 1, Part 2 and gradually "fill" your table of contents with text. Or why not make a more detailed book order for yourself to follow, similar to the one that would be needed if you hired a ghostwriter. Having a clear plan makes it easier to know what needs to be done, which in turn makes it easier to get things done.

My impression of writer's block is that many people who struggle to overcome it focus far too much on little tactical no-brainers like putting their phone away and sitting down to write undisturbed for an hour. I think most people already know what they should be doing, which is sitting down and writing, but are actually struggling to deal with that uncomfortable mental resistance that a blank piece of paper can present. But you still have to start somewhere, some word has to be the first, there are no shortcuts around it.

After you've finished writing your book and made it as good as you can, you need an outsider to read it. Even if you have proof read the text countless times and think it is as good as it can be, it can always be improved. It is important that someone who can be honest with you is the reader and that you decide how and with what eyes the person in question will read the book. This is because there is a difference between reading for spelling mistakes and reading to objectively examine how clear/well-structured/easy to read the book is.

Once the text is finished, it's time to start thinking about the book title and cover, two of the most important pieces to make the book sell!

6. Titles and covers that grab the attention of the right customers

The book title, combined with the book cover, is the first thing Amazon's customers see when they scroll through the flow of books. The role of the book title and cover is therefore to attract attention and create an interest in wanting to know more about the book. You can imagine that the book title and cover are at the beginning of the evaluation journey, where Amazon's customers ask themselves questions like; Will this book help me make more money? Make my relationships better? Help me lose weight? The book title and cover must clearly signal the book's niche and then act as a magnet to attract the right type of customer.

In addition to grabbing attention, the book title and cover are also an important piece of the puzzle when readers recommend books to each other. If the book title is easy to remember and the book cover is easy to describe, then the chances increase that readers will recommend the book to other readers and that they in turn will find your book.

Formulating a book title and designing a book cover that captures the interest of the right customers requires both flair and patience. In this chapter, I explain how to formulate the book title and design the book cover correctly.

Most of the time it takes a few tries and some fiddling with different words and designs before it feels right, so don't feel the stress of having to force out a book title and publish the book with a less-than-stellar book cover just to get it out quickly.

A book title consists of two parts

A book title is divided into two parts, a main title and a subtitle. In Amazon publishing, there are two different schools of thought when it comes to setting the main and subtitle. One school believes that the most important thing is to include as many keywords/search phrases in the main title as possible, while the other school is all about the main title just catching attention. Personally, I prefer the latter, using the main title as a way of attracting attention and saving the keywords/search phrases for the subtitle. An exception to that, however, would be if the book title is obviously improved by the inclusion of a keyword in the main title. To show how the book title can be formulated in a good way, I will analyze three different book titles.

Analysis of three book titles

Surrounded by Idiots

An example of a book title where the main title attracts attention while the keywords/search phrases are used in the subtitle is Tomas Eriksson's famous book *Surrounded by Idiots*. Personally, I think Surrounded by Idiots is an attention-grabbing title that makes me want to know more about what the book is about. The subtitle of the same book is *The Four Types of Human Behavior and How to Effectively Communicate with Each in Business (and in Life)*, where the subtitle contains several possible keywords/search phrases. Can you identify any of them?

Keyword/search phrase refers to the word or phrase that Amazon customers type into the search box inside Amazon when searching for books. In this case, "how to", "business", "human behavior", "life" and "communicate" are just some of the keywords/search phrases that appear in the subtitle of Tomas Eriksson's book. If a customer enters one or more of those words in the search box inside Amazon, the book will appear somewhere in the search results. Note that "somewhere" can mean anything from page 1 to page 10, 100 or 200, etc. in the flow of books. I'll write more about what affects where in the flow the book appears and how you can make it appear as high as possible in the flow in Chapter 8.

Speak With No Fear

A second example of a brilliant attention-grabbing title combined with a subtitle containing relevant keywords is the book with the main title _Speak With No Fear_ and the subtitle _Go from a nervous, nauseated, and sweaty speaker to an excited, energized, and passionate presenter._ In this case, it is clear what the book is about and what the book does for the reader. If one of my acute problems/issues had been that I had stage fright about speaking in front of people, I'm sure I would have clicked on that book and started evaluating whether it was a book worth buying.

I Will Teach You to Be Rich

A third and final example of a main title that catches the eye is Ramit Sethi's book _I Will Teach You to Be Rich_. Pretty easy to understand what that book does for the reader, isn't it? Although in some ways this book contains the same information as many other financial and personal finance books on the market, the title _I Will Tech You to Be Rich_ attracts far more attention and interest than if Ramit had named the book "personal finance 101", or something like that. The subtitle of the book is _No Guilt. No Excuses. No BS. Just a 6-Week Program That Works._ In this case, the subtitle does not contain any clear keywords/search phrases. So why doesn't Ramit have the keyword subtitle? One reason is simply because he doesn't rely on Amazon's search results to get traffic to the book and therefore doesn't need to include keywords in the subtitle. He has several hundred thousand people on his email list who trust his advice on finances and he can single-handedly drive enough traffic to the book to kick-start Amazon's algorithms. After all, the rest of us, who can't drive that much traffic to a book on our own, would do best to use the subtitle to include keywords/search phrases and thereby optimize the chances of the book showing up in the search feed.

How to compose a main title that catches the attention of the right customers

When I published one of my own marketing books in May 2021, I followed the same strategy and tried to have a main title that captures attention and a subtitle that contained relevant keywords/search phrases. The common thread in that book is that far too many of those marketing their products/services on social media are focusing on the wrong things. Instead of focusing on how much money they make, most tend to focus on the number of likes, number of followers and how many people share a particular post. To capture that message in an interesting main title, the result was the main title *Likes Don't Pay Bills*, a title that I am happy with and that I can safely say does the job as the book sold well over 1,000 copies during the launch period alone.

When you are working on composing the main title of your own book, I recommend that you first go to Amazon and look around at similar books in the book's niche. Try to put yourself in the perspective of the Amazon customer and imagine that you are one of them, looking for a book to solve a problem in your everyday life. If they are choosing between different books, what would make them interested in your book? It's not always obvious what captures a particular person's interest, but a little trick is to start with the book's common thread and then rephrase it into a short statement that grabs their attention. Then you have a concrete idea that you can start working on and eventually refine into an interesting main title.

How to write a subtitle

Since the main title's job is to grab attention, the subtitle should instead focus on what the book does for the reader. This means that the subtitle should address the reader's questions and describe what results the reader will get from reading the book and how the reader's life will be better in some way. The subtitle also acts, in a way, as an extension of the main title and further clarifies the niche in which the book is.

When I was working on the subtitle for my book Likes Don't Pay Bills, I first thought of using the subtitle "Five Social Media Marketing Myths", as the book contains a lot of information about various myths in social media marketing. However, when I asked for feedback on the subtitle from established authors, it became clear that "Five Social Media Marketing Myths" did not clearly communicate what the reader would get out of reading the book. I then changed the subtitle to *How to Leverage Social Media to Get Leads and Customers*, which better matches the readers' most pressing issues and more clearly describes the benefits and results readers will get from reading the book. The subtitle thereby also included several relevant keywords/search phrases, more on that shortly.

If you look at the subtitles I gave as examples in the analysis above, *"The Four Types of Human Behavior and How to Effectively Communicate with Each in Business (and in Life)"*, *"Go from a nervous, nauseated, and sweaty speaker to an excited, energized, and passionate"* and *"No Guilt. No Excuses.*

No BS. Just a 6-Week Program That Works", you will see that all of them clearly and specifically describe what the reader will get out of reading one of those books.

Include keywords in the subtitle

The subtitle has an additional purpose beyond describing the benefits readers will derive from reading the book. It should contain one or more keywords/search phrases to help the book appear when Amazon customers use the search box inside Amazon to find books. Therefore, when composing the book's subtitle, it is smart to include one or more of the keywords you used when researching your book ideas earlier. You already know that there is a demand for that type of book, so if you try to include one or more of the keywords/search phrases in the subtitle (or the main title if you think it fits better there), your book will show up when a reader searches for any of those words inside Amazon. The important thing is just that the subtitle flows well and feels natural. If you include too many keywords (also known as "keyword stuffing"), the subtitle can feel heavy and difficult to read, and then it can easily have the opposite effect.

Design a book cover that makes the book sell

When I started Amazon publishing and was about to order my first book cover, I was advised that the most important thing of all was that the cover stood out. As Amazon customers scrolled through all the books, the book cover should shine like a star in the night and be a contrast that stands out from the noise. Makes sense, doesn't it? It's just a problem. When it comes to book covers, the advice is wrong. A book cover shouldn't stand out. It should fit in, within the confines of the niche, as we humans are automatically drawn to things we recognize and away from things that feel alien.

As an example, let's say you want to publish a financial book. The purpose of the book cover will be to attract readers interested in economics and make them want to know more about the book, which only works if the cover looks like an economics book cover is supposed to look like. The book cover in this case should therefore fit within the framework of what a reader interested in economics would expect an economics book cover to look like. If the cover of the book instead stands out, for example by having a picture of a tree or some other irrelevant motif on the cover, there is a high risk that people looking for economics books will not understand that the book is about economics and will therefore scroll past it.

Whether the cover is "good-looking" or not is of less importance. The most important thing is that it looks professional, which is not always the same thing as "good-looking". One pitfall of trying to make "good-looking" book covers is that it is a subjective judgement whether a book cover is good-looking or not. If two people look at a book cover and one person loves it while the other person doesn't like it at all, which is true? After all, it's the same cover.

A recurring theme in this book is to see the world from the perspective of Amazon's customers, and when it comes to book covers, that is very much true. To produce a cover that fits within your book's niche, while still looking professional and attracting the right readers, here's what you do:

Go to Amazon and click through until you get to one of your book's categories. We can play with the idea that your book is in economics. Then go to the overall category for economics books where the top 100 best-selling economics books are listed. Look carefully at all the book covers and try to form an opinion about whether there are any commonalities between the different covers. For example, a common denominator might be that certain colors are used more than others or that certain types of symbols or illustrations are used on the covers. Also note whether the cover contains mainly text or whether there are pictures, and if so, what kind of pictures. The purpose of this is not to copy all other covers, but rather to get a general idea of what Amazon's customers expect a financial book cover to look like. Designing your book cover in the same pattern means that when Amazon's customers scroll through the flow of books and see your book, they will immediately see that it is a financial book.

Three ways to make a professional book cover
Depending on your budget and design skills, there are different ways to make a book cover. For example, you can design it yourself in a design program like Canva. A budget option is to order a cover from Fiverr for $5-$20 and an option for those with a larger budget is to start a book cover contest on 99designs, which costs from $199 depending on how big of a contest you want to make.

Create your own cover in Canva
Considering how incredibly important the cover is, my recommendation is to get help designing the cover. The imminent risk of designing the cover yourself is not that it won't look good, but rather that it won't signal the right message, which in turn means that the right readers won't find the cover interesting. If you still feel you want to try designing yourself, you can do so in a design program such as Canva, based on the research you've done on book covers in that niche.

Hire a designer on Fiverr

At fiverr.com, you can hire a cover designer for cheap. Open an account on Fiverr, browse around until you find one that looks good, and place an order. The important thing if you decide to hire a cover designer on Fiverr is that you compile your cover research into a clear order and send in examples of book covers that you think would suit your book. If you're lucky, you might get back a really professional cover, but you might just as easily be unlucky and get back a cover that looks unprofessional and homemade.

Organise a book cover competition on 99 designs

99designs (99designs.com) is a site where you can organize a cover competition where different designers post their entries and progressively refine them according to your ongoing feedback. Usually, a competition lasts for a couple of days. The designer who wins the contest gets the prize money. On 99 designs, the way it works is that you upload all the information about your book and what your cover preferences are, then you choose how many designers you want to be in the competition. The cheapest option is $199 at the time of this writing and then you're guaranteed 30 different covers. The quality varies a lot, but in my eyes it's still considerably higher than the covers from Fiverr.

Some final thoughts on book covers

However you choose to produce the book cover, the goal is to signal the right message and look professional. All so that Amazon's customers will find it interesting enough to want to know more about the book and click through to the book's product page. Do the best you can in this situation. You can always change the book cover afterwards, even after the book has been published on Amazon. Once you've made the book cover, it's almost time to start preparing the book for publication, but first a chapter on how Amazon's customers buy books.

7. Amazon customers' buying journey

Before it's time to publish your book, let me tell you a little about how Amazon customers behave when they shop for books. This is to give you a better idea of all the different steps Amazon customers usually go through before they decide to buy a particular book. When you have an overview of the buying journey, it's easier to see how all the elements of your book fit together to help Amazon's customers find the book and then hopefully buy it. To have a picture in front of you of how the buying journey works, you can again go to Amazon and look for a book similar to your upcoming book and click into that book's product page. The product page is the page where customers can read the book description, click through to "look inside" and read the book's reviews, and more.

Now imagine that you are a potential customer and that you have been browsing around Amazon for a while and have come across the book you have in front of you. What would make you buy that particular book? How can you know for sure that this is the book you want to read and that it will give you the answers you are looking for? Think about those questions for a moment.

Based on my own behavior when I buy books on Amazon, which I think is pretty consistent with the behavior of most Amazon customers, it is rare that I buy a completely unknown book the first time I come across it. If I do, it's usually because the book has captured my interest with a superb cover or a clear title that signals that the book contains the answer to one of my most pressing questions at the time. The exception is possibly if the book is so cheap that I think it's worth taking a chance and buying it regardless of whether it's good or bad.

Although I rarely get hooked and buy a book the first time I come across it, I'm pretty sure that my subconscious still puts a lot of books in my memory. The more often I'm on Amazon looking for books, the more often I see the same cover. Eventually, I recognize several of the books that show up in my Amazon feed, and that in turn causes me to put some of them on my watch list. When I go through the watch list, I usually click through to the product pages of the books and once there, I usually behave like this: First I skim the book description to get a feel for whether the book is for me at all. If the book description is interesting, I usually scroll down to the book's reviews and read what others think of the book. Then I read a paragraph from the introduction, evaluate if the price is right, and either buy the book or click away.

When it comes to reading, my ambition is to read a couple of books a month, which means I'm always on the lookout for new books. This in turn means that I'm not very "picky" when it comes to buying books. If a book seems interesting, I buy it. If it turns out later that the book is not good at all, then I just stop reading and buy another book instead.

Once you have published your book, it will have its own product page on Amazon, just like any other book there. This means that just as you evaluate the book you have in front of you now, and just as I evaluate the books I buy, so too will Amazon's customers evaluate whether your book is right for them.

The clues on Amazon's product pages

If you look again at the product page you have in front of you, but instead of just looking at it you ask yourself the question *why?* to everything you see. Why is the book cover on the left of the product page instead of the right? Why is there a "read more" button after the fifth line of the e-book's description? Why are those particular books shown in the "Also bought" feed? Why is there no buy button at the end of the book description? Why is there a buy button at the end of the "look inside"?

What do you think?

Amazon has never said it themselves, but a book's product page is a direct reflection of how Amazon customers behave when shopping for books. It's no coincidence that the product page looks the way it does; it looks that way for a reason. Why is the book cover on the left instead of the right? It has to do with the way our eyes move when we look at a screen, as we usually look at the top left corner first. Why is there a "read more" button after the fifth line of the e-book's description? Well, because most customers don't read more than five lines of the book description before deciding whether the book is still interesting and Amazon wants to make the buying journey as smooth as possible for its customers. Why is there no buy button at the end of the book description? Well, because customers are in the middle of their buying journey and are still evaluating whether they want to buy the book or not. Why does Amazon display the specific also bought books on that particular book? Well, because Amazon is doing everything they can to match the right book with the right reader. Why is there a buy button at the end of "look inside"? Well, because once a potential customer has read all the text in "look inside" they are usually ready to buy the book. So, a buy button at this particular point matches where customers are in their buying journey.

How the book sales funnel works

A common concept in business is the *sales funnel*. A sales funnel is defined as all the different steps a potential customer takes on the journey from prospect to paying customer. Usually, the sales funnel is visualized by a funnel-like image, where the number of potential customers gets fewer and fewer, but gets closer and closer to a purchase, the further down the funnel they get.

An example of a sales funnel might be 400 people attending an author's free open lecture, where the author in question hopes to sell books and courses at the end of the lecture. In such an example, there are 400 potential customers at the top of the sales funnel who, in that situation, probably lack a direct desire to buy. Let's say that out of the 400 potential customers, 40 people find the lecture interesting enough to decide to buy the author's book. And of the 40 who buy the book, five also sign up for one of the author's courses. The sales funnel in this simplified example then shows that out of 400 potential customers, 40 became paying customers, five of whom are premium customers.

How the sales funnel is relevant to Amazon publishing

To make it easier to see how the sales funnel is highly relevant to Amazon publishing, let's make up a fictional example with a person we call Bob. So here we look at the sales funnel from the perspective of a specific customer. Bob has an urgent problem, namely that he wants to lose weight and get in shape.

So, after some time of thinking back and forth, Bob has decided to lose weight. He is currently at the top of the sales funnel and has no immediate desire to buy a specific book at the moment. Bob is Googling and watching YouTube clips to learn more about exercise and health. A few weeks go by and Bob finds a podcast where he thinks the guy who has the podcast, Mike, seems like a reasonable guy and Bob feels he can relate to most of what Mike says. Bob starts following the podcast and even catches up on old episodes. Time and time again, Bob hears Mike recommend the *Get Fit* exercise book, which makes Bob curious to know more about the book. Bob browses Amazon, searches for Get Fit and starts reading about the book. Now Bob has slipped much further down the sales funnel.

Bob is now on the product page for Get Fit. He's evaluating whether the book is right for him, but something's not right. Bob is a man in his 50s and Get Fit seems to be a general exercise book, aimed at both girls and guys of all ages and Bob can't quite relate. He drops his thoughts on Get Fit and begins the hunt for another, for him, more specific book. After some searching, Bob spots the cover of your book *How Men Get Fit in Their 50s*. Bingo! thinks Bob and clicks through to the product page.

Once on your book's product page, he reads the book description and "look inside" where he sees several chapter headings that catch his interest. After that, he reads some of the book's reviews, drags his mouse cursor to the buy button, ready to pull the trigger. He thinks for a few more seconds before pressing buy. In this way, Bob has passed all the way down the sales funnel that led to his purchase of your book.

Now, if the book delivers what Bob expects (or more), you've almost certainly got a lifelong fan who will recommend *How Men Get Fit in Their 50s* to his buddy Robert, who also wants to get fit. Robert buys the book without blinking, as Bob explains how much the book has helped him solve his weight problem and get in shape.

But what is really going on in this example?

Bob goes through a journey where he becomes aware of his problem and starts looking for a solution. Once he knows how he wants to solve his problem (by reading a book) he begins his buying journey and after some searching ends up in a sales funnel that leads to your book and where all the elements in terms of cover, description and "look inside" worked together to make Bob take the step to buy the book. So in this case, the book is at the bottom of the sales funnel and is the solution to Bob's problem. This is where you want your book to be. At the bottom of the sales funnel and the solution to as many customers' problems as possible. Keep this in mind now that it's high time for you to publish your own book!

8. Prepare your book for publication

In a way, publishing a book on Amazon is like putting together a puzzle. The puzzle in this case consists of the text, the book cover, the book description, the metadata and a number of other pieces that all need to be prepared and fit together to make the puzzle go as smoothly as possible. In this chapter, we'll look at how to prepare all the pieces of the puzzle so that the book has the best chance of a successful launch.

Write an enticing introduction to the book

In the example with Bob in the last chapter, I wrote about how Bob evaluated the fictional book *How Men Get Fit in Their 50s* and whether it contained the answer to his pressing questions. To make sure it did, Bob read the table of contents and the introduction to the book, among other things. Both the table of contents and the introduction were available in the "look inside" view, and what Bob could read there was a direct factor in him actually buying the book. In other words, now that you are preparing your own book for publication, it is extremely important that you polish the text that will appear in the "look inside" view, as it is an important piece of the puzzle that has a major impact on sales.

When I write the introductions to my books, I always think extra carefully about what the readers deep down want answers to and how the book delivers them. An example is my book *Likes Don't Pay Bills*, which is a book about social media marketing. After researching the book's target audience, it became clear that the readers I was writing to wanted to learn how to get customers and make money on social media. Once I knew what the book's target audience was looking for,

I was able to adapt introduction accordingly, writing like this in the first two paragraphs of the introduction:

Your customers are on social media. They are probably scrolling their feeds right now, as you are reading this. How can I know that? Because everyone's customers are on social media, all the time.

With the right strategies, you can get their attention, connect with them, and build relationships with them. However, with the wrong strategies, they will scroll right past your posts, and your attempt to use social media as a marketing tool can be a frustrating time-sink.

In addition to the introduction, the table of contents, containing all the book's chapter headings, is also visible in the look inside view. Therefore, it may be a good idea to name the chapter headings something that hooks the book's target audience. This could be in the form of answers to common questions. Think about whether the chapter headings in your book are hooking enough and if not, rewrite them to make them more compelling.

I want to stress that the example from my book above is in no way a recipe for how to write an introduction, but it can certainly be used as inspiration when writing the introduction to your book, or as a helping hand if you are guiding the ghostwriter to write it.

When it comes to introductions, I would also like to mention a common mistake many Amazon publishers make when writing their introductions. It's not uncommon to be recommended to use the look inside view as a way to capture potential customers' contact information. Usually, this involves including links pointing *away* from the book and product page in the form of links to a landing page, website or social media.

Put yourself in the shoes of a potential customer. The potential customer is interested in buying a book and has clicked all the way to "look inside". Once there, almost ready to buy the book, they are given the choice to click from there to another place and perform another action in the form of signing up to an email list or following a social media account, for example. It's almost a bit like being candy-hungry, going to a candy store, filling your candy bag to the brim, walking up to the cashier to pay, and once there, the cashier tries to convince you that you should consider buying *ice cream* instead, and in a different *store* at that. How would you have felt then? I guess you would have been a bit confused and maybe felt a lot of resistance to buying anything at all. And it works the same way inside Amazon. The slightest bit of resistance or upheaval in the sales funnel can be the difference between a potential customer clicking "buy with 1-click" or them leaving the product page never to return.

How to write a professional end to the book
Now we leave the introduction to the book and move swiftly to the final word, which is just as important a piece of the puzzle as the introduction. Imagine the last time you read a really good book or saw a really good movie. When the book or movie was over, what did you want? If you're like me, you wanted more. After I've spent hours reading a book, thinking and reflecting on what message the author wants to convey and how I can apply it to my own life, I almost get a little separation anxiety when the book is over. But the end of a book doesn't really have to be the end. It can also be the beginning of the next book.

Using the end of a book as a springboard to the next book can boost sales significantly. Since everyone who reads the end of the book has automatically already invested time in the book, they probably also have a good sense of whether your next book is for them, and there's no need for an over-the-top sales pitch to try to convince them to buy it. All that's needed is to make it easy for readers to find where you want to lead them. In the e-book you can add a hyperlink and, in the paperback, you can write short, simple instructions on how to find them. Even if you haven't published more than one book, it's still smart to use the end of the book to ask readers to perform an action, which could be asking them to sign up for your newsletter, follow you on social media or leave a review on the book. Just be careful not to ask readers for too much at the end of the book, as it's easy for multiple choices to create confusion and have the opposite effect. I usually recommend a maximum of two options, suggesting to lead them to the next book and to sign up to my mailing list.

An example of a closing statement (which I kind of "stole" from Robert Ryan's book *Author Unleashed*), in which I try to get the reader to leave a review of my book Likes Don't Pay Bills, might look like this:

There are plenty of great marketing books online, so thank you for choosing Likes Don't Pay Bills and reading all the way to the end!

What I hate after reading a book is the feeling that it's stuffed with bad and boring content that's easily found for free online. If I gave you that, let me know in the reviews. On the other hand, If I gave you what you expected (or more), please tell me that in the reviews!

How to format the book

Once you've written hooky chapter headings, a salesy introductory text and a closing word to lead readers on, it's time to format the text into an e-book and a paperback. You probably have your text file in a writing program like Word or Pages, or you may have used a more professional program like Scrivener. Depending on which program you use, the formatting process may be different. Here I will give you *general* guidelines on how to format, based on Word. I recommend that you google or search on Youtube for more information and help on how to format the book in the particular program you are using. Remember that when you format the book, it is only the text file that is being formatted and you should not put the book cover or the book description in the text file.

Step one in formatting is to decide what size you want the book to be. I have the same paper size for both the e-book and the paperback. Generally speaking, I let the paperback dictate what size I want the book to be, with a common size being 6 * 9 inches (22.86 cm * 15.24 cm). To change the paper size and get the book in the size you want, do this in Word: go to Layout → Size → More paper sizes and enter the height and width. If you are not sure which size to choose, check the KDP website to see what sizes are available. One thing to keep in mind when deciding what size you want is that you can't change the size after you've published the book. The reason why I want the same paper size for the e-book as for the paperback is because Amazon shows how many pages the book is. If you then have the e-book as A4 size, it will look like the e-book has fewer pages than the paperback, which can be confusing for Amazon's customers.

Step two in formatting is to embellish the text to the extent you want to make the reading experience better. For example, you can make anchors or have a different font for the chapter headings than for the rest of the text.

Once you have decided on the size you want the book to be and have embellished the text as you wish, it's time to format an e-book and a paperback. There a couple of things that differ between e-books and paperbacks that might be useful to keep in mind along the way.

Prepare the e-book file for publishing

An e-book is usually read on an e-book tablet, such as a Kindle e-reader. Depending on the type of e-book tablet the reader has, the amount of text on the screen varies. An e-book also allows you to zoom in on the text. The text in an e-book is therefore "floating", which means that an e-book should not have page numbers. So, when you format your e-book, you should remove all page numbers. Another specific feature of e-books is that you can include links in the book. This could be a link to your website or a link to one of your other books.

Once your text document for the e-book contains everything you want to include, you'll need to convert the text file to an *e-pub* file. This can be done in different ways. By the time you read this, it is possible that Word also has a built-in e-pub conversion, as Google DOCs have. You can therefore start by checking whether this feature is available in your writing program. If not, there are other ways to convert your Word document to an e-pub file. Either you can buy the service from a freelancer, buy a formatting and conversion program, or you can use a free conversion tool. One free tool I have used myself and been happy with can be found (at the time of writing) here: https://convertio.co/doc-epub.

Once you've converted the text file to an e-pub file, it's ready to be published!

Prepare the paperback for publication

When formatting the paperback, you should include page numbers and it should not have any hyperlinks. Also, keep in mind that the page break for subheadings must be neat, so that a subheading, for example, does not end up at the bottom of a page. When you have finished formatting, save the file as a PDF and check that everything looks as you intended. Once the PDF looks the way you want it to, it's ready to publish too!

How to write an engagning book description

The book description is the text about the book that Amazon customers can read on the book's product page. To be able to write a good and interesting book description, it helps to know what the book description does in the sales funnel I wrote about earlier. A clue about the book description's task that Amazon gives us is that a potential customer is usually not ready to buy a book only after they have read the book description. How do I know that? Well because if it were, Amazon would have placed a buy button at the end of the book description. The lack of a buy button at the end of the book description cannot be interpreted in any other way than that when the customer reads the book description, they are still in the evaluation phase and are evaluating whether the book they have in front of them is right for them or not.

Another clue that strengthens this hypothesis is that just below the book description, inside the product pages, Amazon displays a carousel of other books. This means that if a potential customer reads the book description for a book, but doesn't find it enticing enough, the customer has a buffet of other similar books in plain sight and can easily click through and check out the next book. All to keep the customer's interest and lead them to an actual purchase.

So what can we learn from this and how can we use this knowledge? It is clear to me that the job of the book description is not necessarily to sell the book, but rather to ensure that a potential customer does not lose interest in the book and click away from the book's product page. Not only that, but the book description has to be compelling enough to make the potential customer want to know more about the book, for example by clicking through to the "look inside" view or the book's reviews.

The formula for writing compelling book descriptions
A text that is intended to capture the interest of a potential customer and make them perform a certain action is called "copywriting" text, or just "copy". Writing a book description is a form of copywriting. In order to be successful with a book description, I usually recommend using the AIDA copywriting formula. AIDA stands for attention, interest, desire and action.

AIDA is designed in such a way that each step builds on the previous one. This means that in order to succeed in getting a customer to perform a certain desirable action, such as staying on the book's product page, the book description needs to keep the customer's attention (attention), get the customer more interested in the book (interest), gradually get the customer more emotionally invested (desire) and finally get the customer to start reading in the "look inside" view (action).

Once Amazon's customers read the first few lines of the book description, the book cover and/or title must somehow have already captured their interest, otherwise they would never have had the opportunity to read the book description, since the book description is only visible inside the product page, which is accessed by clicking on the book cover or title. This means that the first line of the book description does not have to try to "break through the clutter" in any way. That job has already been done by the book cover and/or title. Instead, the first line of the book description should keep the potential customer's attention. One way to do that is to use an open-ended question or statement that the customer perceives as authentic and recognizable.

An example of an open-ended question in a book description is how I open the book description for my book *Likes Don't Pay Bills*. There I write "Want to learn how to find new clients, sell more products, and make more money using social media?" and my goal with the open-ended question is simply to keep the potential customer's attention. Then the book description must quickly move to building interest and getting the potential customer more and more interested in the book.

Writing copywriting texts that produce the desired results takes a little practice. A basic tip is to start with how the book's target audience expresses itself, what words they use, what concepts are significant to that particular audience, and so on. Using the same words and concepts in the copy that the target group itself uses strengthens the credibility of the book while making the copy appear more authentic. It also helps in the interest/desire phases, where it is important to press the right emotional buttons so that the copy is not perceived as "salesy" or manipulative.

Call to actions for book descriptions

Last but not least comes the "action" part of the book description. In copywriting, this is called a *call to action*, or CTA. A CTA is usually a call to action. If you look around, you'll see CTAs everywhere, in every context. Buy now! Leave a comment! Sign up here! Which are all examples of CTAs.

Many copywriters love CTAs more than anything else. They can talk for hours about what a well-worded CTA can accomplish. What many forget is that as good as a CTA is, it alone can't do all the work. It relies on the pull of everything that comes before it. A misplaced CTA is a bit like walking into a restaurant and the first thing the waiter asks is what you thought of the food. How are you supposed to know? You haven't even seen the menu yet! A misplaced CTA can also be perceived as manipulative as it leaves no room for the customer to think for themselves.

The trick to writing a well-functioning CTA at the end of a book description is for it to act as an invisible helping hand that leads the potential customer further along the evaluation journey. When I write CTAs for my books, I usually use something called a "soft CTA". A soft CTA is a soft prompt, sometimes in the form of an open-ended question, that is intended to keep a potential customer's attention on the book and move them further down the sales funnel on their own, thereby continuing to evaluate whether the book is right for them.

Analysis of the book description for Likes Don't Pay Bills

To try to make it clearer how AIDA works in practice and to help you understand how you can write your own book description using AIDA, we'll look at and analyze the book description for my book

Likes Don't Pay Bills together. I have divided the book description according to AIDA and written the book description in italics with my comments directly below.

The Attention part:
Want to learn how to find new clients, sell more products, and make more money using social media?

Here I try to keep the potential customer's attention to want to read further. Remember that anyone reading this open-ended question must have already clicked through to the product page, which means that the cover and/or title has already caught their attention. While trying to keep their attention, I also try to include some of the target audience's desires that I (thanks to my research) know they have.

The Interest part:
Most social media marketing strategies are designed to inflate useless metrics such as likes, shares, and comments. These metrics might look cool, but they won't grow your business.

In this book, I bust the five most common social media marketing myths and show you how to use social media to your advantage. You'll learn:

how to find your target audience on social media
how to use social media to trigger word of mouth marketing
how to get your target audience attention (crash course in copywriting)
how to build a connection with your audience and earn their trust
how to use social media to grow your email list (email marketing 101)
and of course, how to sell your product/service/offer to your target audience

The idea of the opening sentence in the interest section is that the reader should feel that this is not another book in a series of books that focus on just getting lots of likes and followers, but rather a book about how the reader can make money from their social media. Next, I describe what readers get out of reading the book so that they can also get an idea of whether the book is for them or not. The line between interest and desire is thus somewhat blurred here.

The Desire part:
The strategies I talk about in this book work for all social media platforms, and it doesn't matter if you have 50 or 50K followers.

A clarification that the strategies in the book work for all platforms and for everyone, regardless of how many followers you have. Here I have deliberately written "50K" instead of "50,000", as many people in the book's target group express follower numbers in the unit "K". Such seemingly small things are what create recognition and relevance.

The Action part:
Ready to unleash the true power of social media marketing?

A "soft CTA" in the form of an open-ended question. Here I am not saying "buy now!!!", but I am trying to lead the reader to continue evaluating the book, which hopefully leads to a purchase further down the sales funnel.

Write the book description for your book
Now it's time for you to write a book description for your book. If you have used a ghostwriter who has already written the book

description, my recommendation is that you revise it based on the AIDA formula.

When writing the book description, a tip is to copy your book cover and paste it into your text document, so that you can see the cover in front of you at all times when writing the book description. You want the book cover and the book description to signal the same thing and by looking at the cover when you write the book description you will achieve this more easily. Another tip is to divide the description according to AIDA and write one part at a time. Once you have written all the parts, put them together and only then start filing the whole thing so that the text flows the way you want it to.

How to find the right keywords for the book
We leave the book description and move on to another important piece of the puzzle, namely keywords! One way that Amazon customers use to find books they want to read is by searching the search box located at the top of the Amazon homepage. You can search for book titles, author names, keywords, search phrases and basically anything. After a search, Amazon presents a feed of books relevant to that particular search. The keywords associated with your book can therefore determine whether or not a potential customer finds your book in the feed.

When choosing which keywords to associate with the book, there are a few things to consider. Inside your KDP account (more on KDP in Chapter 9), there will be seven different boxes where you can enter up to 50 characters in each box. According to Amazon's guidelines for how keywords work, it is sufficient to type a keyword once in a keyword box. I've done several tests to confirm that what Amazon says about keywords in this case is correct, and it is.

I've found that if an Amazon customer searches for "yoga back pain" and you have the keyword "yoga" in one of your keyword boxes and the keywords "back" and "pain" in two of your other keyword boxes, Amazon will pull keywords from all of your keyword boxes to match what the customer searched for. This means you never have to repeat a keyword, and you can fill all seven boxes with unique words. The more relevant keywords you have added to your book, the more likely customers are to find it.

Another thing to consider is to include filler words and sentence builders in the keyword boxes. If a customer searches for "books about yoga", "how to do yoga" or "yoga books for seniors", you want to include the keywords *about*, *how to* and *for* as some of the book's keywords so that the book will appear in the customer's search result.

For inspiration on what keywords to associate with your book, browse similar books on Amazon and try to gather 15-25 different keywords relevant to your book. Think about how you think customers on Amazon search for books like your upcoming book. One tip is to start by typing a keyword into the search box on Amazon, then Amazon will automatically suggest what other keywords customers have searched for. You can include these other keywords as one of your keywords, provided of course that the keyword is also relevant to your book.

Include the book in up to ten categories
On Amazon, there are over 13,000 different book categories. When you publish your book, you can include it in two of them. Not much, is it?! But fortunately, you have the option to include the book in eight more categories *after* the book has been published. Having the

book in a total of ten different categories instead of two can make a big difference to sales as the book will appear in more places inside Amazon. You can already look up ten relevant categories for your book. If you can't find ten relevant categories, fewer is fine too.

There are several different routes to Amazon's category list. One way is to click to *Kindle Store* → *Kindle eBooks* and from there you can start scanning which categories are relevant to your book. Another way is to go to a book's product page, scroll down to *product details* and click through to that book's categories.

Whichever route you take, you'll know you're in the right place as soon as you're in a top 100 list, as each category has its own top 100 list. So, there are more than 13,000 top 100 lists on Amazon! In addition to a top 100 list, each category also has a "new release" list, which is of particular interest to you if you've just published your book.

Once you have published your book, it will be on the new release list for each category for 30 days. The new release lists also have their own top 100 list and usually it only takes a couple of sales for your book to sail up as #1 new release in any of the book's ten categories. When the book becomes #1 new release, its product page receives an orange flag signaling that the book is a #1 new release. Having that flag on the product page gives more weight to the book and can help more customers buy the book.

When publishing the book, my recommendation is to choose the two most relevant categories you can find. This inclusion of your book in a total of ten categories is not something that Amazon advertises or makes clear when you publish the book. Once the book has gone live you need to email KDP support, which is done from within your KDP account, and ask to include the book in additional categories. If you wish, you can keep the two categories you chose at the time of publication and include the book in eight more. The only important thing is that you must specify the entire category chain when you email KDP support. The full category chain means all levels of categories and you can see them on the left side of the screen inside Amazon if you are browsing from a computer (the category chain is not visible in mobile mode). An example of what the category chain looks like for the category "Budgeting & Money Management" is *Kindle eBooks/Business & Money/Personal Finance/Budgeting & Money Management.*

Last piece of the puzzle, make a back cover for the paperback
The last piece of the puzzle before publication is to make a paperback cover. A paperback book has a two-page cover (a front and a back). Contact your cover designer, send them the e-book cover and ask them to make a paperback cover. What the designer needs to know is the size of the paperback, how many pages the book is and the text you want on the back of the book. My recommendation is that you use the book description as the text for the back of the book.

After you've prepared all the pieces, it's time to piece them together and make the book available for sale on Amazon!

9. Publish the book on Amazon

In previous chapters I have referred to the KDP on a couple of occasions. KDP is an acronym for *Kindle Direct Publishing* and is Amazon's platform for self-publishing e-books, paperbacks and physical hardcovers. The web address for KDP is www.kdp.com. In order to publish your books on Amazon, you need to open an account there.

Start by going to KDP and opening an account in your real name (do not open the account under your pseudonym even if you are going to publish the book under one). Although your KDP account is opened under your real name, it will never appear publicly on Amazon. Amazon's customers will never be able to track that you are the publisher of a particular book. Opening a KDP account is completely free and there is no cost to publish one or more books. And for those of you with businesses, it's perfectly possible to open a business account on KDP. It is also possible to switch from a personal account to a business account should you wish to do so in the future.

Your KDP account is the hub of everything related to book publishing on Amazon. It's from KDP that you publish your books, make changes to your books, manage metadata, and more. It's also where you specify where you want your royalty payments to go. Personally, I handle my KDP account as carefully as I handle my bank accounts. This means that I would never give out my password to my KDP account or allow anyone else to log in to my KDP account.

Taxes

I often get questions about how to tax and declare your Amazon income. As I am not trained in tax law and therefore do not feel comfortable advising on tax issues, I usually refer to always contacting the Tax Agency. The Tax Agency can tell you what to do based on your particular circumstances, whether you publish your books as a private individual, a sole proprietorship or through a limited company.

Whether you publish your books as an individual or through a company, you will be required to complete a digital tax interview when you open your KDP account. The tax interview consists of a series of written questions.

Publish the e-book

Now it's finally time to publish the e-book! In the last chapter, we prepared all the pieces needed to make the publishing process as smooth as possible. The first time you publish an e-book, it will probably take some time, so be prepared for that. If you get stuck during the publishing process, there's a help center with great instructions and videos inside KDP to get you started, so check it out. Here's a general explanation of how all the different steps in the publishing process work.

Start by logging in to your KDP account and go to "Bookshelf". At the top of the page, it says "+ Create", click there and select "Kindle Book". This will take you to the steps where you will fill in all the details about the book. Once you have published the book, it will appear under "your Books". Later, when you want to publish the paperback, you can press "+ Create paperback" within the book's box in "your Books". If you do this, you will not have to fill in all the information about the book again and the publication of the paperback will be a snap.

Title, subtitle, and author

Enter the language, title, subtitle and author name of the e-book. Be sure to spell it correctly and make sure it matches what's on the cover.

Description

Description is the same as book description. Copy and paste the book description and format it so that it looks good. A tip is to have the first line of the book description (the attention part) in bold, as bold contrasts with Amazon's white product pages and attracts the eyes of Amazon's customers. Also, try to make the book description a little airy so that it is easy to read.

Publishing Rights

Check the box to indicate that you own the rights to the book. If you have written the book yourself or used a ghostwriter through The Writing Summit, you own 100% of all rights. If you have used another ghostwriter, you will most likely own all the rights, but it is worth double-checking just in case.

Keywords

In the last chapter I wrote about how to find keywords. Remember that you don't have to repeat words and not to forget to include sentence builders like "about" and "how to". Fill the boxes to the brim with different words and phrases relevant to the book. As an example, I filled in the first keyword box for my book Likes Don't

Pay Bills like this: "social media marketing for business guide" (note that there doesn't have to be a comma between the keywords).

Categories

Here you select the two most relevant categories for your book that you find. After the book has been published, email KDP and ask to have the book included in up to eight additional categories, which I wrote more about in the last chapter.

Upload the book file and cover

When you get to the step where you upload the text file, you will see that it is possible to upload the e-book in several different formats, including as a word file. Although it is possible to upload word files, my recommendation is to still publish e-books as an e-pub file. Be careful that you upload the right file so that you don't accidentally publish the wrong version of the book. The cover is uploaded as a jpeg for the e-book and as a PDF for the paperback.

KDP Select

Amazon's subscription service for those who like to read e-books is called Kindle Unlimited. Like many other subscription services, Kindle Unlimited provides unlimited access to a certain range of books. In this case, paying $10 a month means that you have access to all the e-books included in Kindle Unlimited, which is over a million in number.

As an Amazon publisher, you have the option to include your e-book in Kindle Unlimited by checking the box for "enroll in KDP Select". By doing so, you commit that the e-book is exclusive to Amazon for a KDP Select period of 90 days. The e-book being exclusive on

Amazon means that you promise that you will not sell the e-book anywhere else during the time the book is included in KDP Select.

After 90 days, the next KDP Select period starts automatically, for another 90 days. If you do not want to keep the e-book in KDP Select, you need to go in and end the KDP Select period by clicking on "KDP Select info" which you can find by hovering over the three dots in the "your books" view. There you can unsubscribe the e-book from KDP Select. Just remember that you may not publish the e-book anywhere else until the current KDP Select period has expired.

So what would you get out of including your e-book in KDP Select and thereby also having it in Kindle Unlimited? The main advantage of including the book in KDP Select is that you can earn royalties in two different ways on the same e-book. First, you earn royalties when Amazon customers purchase the e-book and second, you earn royalties when Kindle Unlimited subscribers read the e-book as part of their subscription.

Royalties from Kindle Unlimited are calculated once a month. All publishers who have at least one e-book included in Kindle Unlimited are eligible to share in a monthly pot. The pot is based on how many subscribers are included in Kindle Unlimited that month, and as a reference, the monthly pot is usually in the tens of millions of dollars. Royalties are calculated based on how many pages readers have read of your e-books relative to the total number of pages read for all e-books in Kindle Unlimited. As an average, a page read equals about 5 cents. That means you earn about $1 for every 200 pages read.

Including the e-book in KDP Select also gives you access to a couple of different marketing tools, such as offering the e-book for free for 5 days during each KDP Select period or running various promotions with price reductions on the e-book.

For myself, only about 5% of my total royalties tend to come from Kindle Unlimited, which is quite natural given that Kindle Unlimited is designed primarily for Amazon customers who read fiction and for publishers who publish long fiction books.

It's up to you to decide whether KDP Select is for your e-book or not, but my recommendation is to include the e-book in KDP Select in the first place, unless you already know that you intend to publish the e-book elsewhere, such as Apple Books, Google or Kobo.

Preview

Once you have filled in all the fields and uploaded all the files, the book is almost ready to be published. But before you press the button and let your e-book go live, you need to do one last thing: open the e-book and check it in preview mode. Preview mode is a reflection of how the finished e-book will look to customers. Browse through the preview, test all the links and check to make sure everything looks good. If there is anything you are unsure about or want to change, now is the time to do it. You don't want to risk the book getting a bad review on something you could have fixed.

Pricing of the e-book

You decide the price of your e-book. My recommendation is that you initially launch the book for 99 cents with a 35% royalty. With 99 cents pricing, you won't earn any significant amount of royalties, but that's not the idea either. The idea is to have as small a threshold between the e-book and Amazon's customers as possible. Only when you have had a dozen sales and a few reviews of your e-book is it time to raise the price, then suggestively to $2.99. Another argument for launching the e-book at 99 cents is that it is a price level that will facilitate marketing via Bookbub (read more about that in Chapter 12).

When setting the price in US dollars, pay attention to how KDP converts the price to other currencies. A book for 99 US cents may have an odd price in other currencies, for example $1.32 in Canadian dollars. Adjust and tweak the price so that it looks commercial in all the different currencies.

After you have completed all the steps in the publishing process, press "publish". It will take about 48 hours until you receive an email that your e-book has been published on Amazon. After you receive the email that the book is published, you can look up the book on Amazon and check the product page to make sure everything looks good. Was your description formatted as you intended? Is everything spelled correctly? If you find something wrong or want to change something, you can easily do so by logging into KDP, changing what you want to change, and republishing the book. If you make changes on the product page or inside the e-book, the old version will remain live until the new one is published.

Some differences when publishing the paperback
After you have published the e-book, it is time to publish the paperback. The process is basically the same. Log in to KDP and start by pressing "+ Create paperback" within the e-book box in "your books". There you will see that some fields are already pre-

filled with the same information you entered when publishing the e-book.

Once you've checked that all the pre-filled information is correct, pull out the paperback book file and cover, upload them and indicate that you want KDP to give you a free ISBN number by pressing "assign me a FREE ISBN". You may not use this ISBN number anywhere else but on KDP.

Preview of the paperback

In order to publish the paperback, you need to make a "preview". Press "launch preview" and see how it looks. Does the book look the way you want it to? If there is something wrong with the book, for example the cover is not the right size, you will get a message about it. You will have to fix any errors that Amazon signals before you can press "Approve Preview" and get to the final step of the publishing process.

Expanded distribution

For paperbacks there is no KDP Select, but Amazon offers "expanded distribution" which means that Amazon can distribute the paperback to other online booksellers if you wish. If you include the paperback in expanded distribution, you may not publish the paperback on other distribution sites such as Ingramspark. I personally do not have any of my paperbacks in Amazon's expanded distribution. Instead, I use Ingramspark to reach online booksellers outside of Amazon because Ingramspark offers both better royalties and wider distribution across more sites than Amazon's expanded distribution.

Pricing and publishing the paperback

You set the price of your paperback. A guideline for a paperback of about 10,000 words is $9.99. Personally, I've never found Amazon customers to be directly price sensitive. This means that a book for $7.99 doesn't necessarily sell better than a book for $9.99 just because it's cheaper. Therefore, I recommend pricing the paperback at $9.99. Later, when you have proof that the paperback is selling, you can try raising the price.

After you have completed all the steps in the publishing process, press "publish". It will take about 48 hours until you receive an email that the paperback is published on Amazon. After you receive the email that the book has been published, you can look it up on Amazon and check the product page to make sure everything looks good. Was your description formatted the way you intended? Is everything spelled correctly? If you find something wrong or want to change something, you can easily do so by logging into KDP, changing what you want to change, and republishing the paperback.

Once both the e-book and the paperback are published, it's time to start marketing and getting the book to sell!

10. Authentic marketing

One of the most common questions in all the author and Amazon publishing groups I'm in is something along the lines of "Hey, can anyone advise on the best way to market my book?".

Before I answer what, in my opinion, are the best ways to market Amazon-published books, I want to share some thoughts I have about the concept of "marketing". In my experience, the concept of marketing raises all kinds of fears and uncomfortable feelings in many people. One contributing reason why this may be so is because it is common to not want to stand out and appear salesy, as many salespeople have a reputation for being sleazy people who are only interested in making money. Who wants to be perceived as a sleazy person who only wants to make money? At least not me! And certainly not you either.

I think it's sad that marketing in many cases has such a bad reputation, but I would argue that it's because people generally lump all types of marketing together and don't distinguish between what is sometimes called manipulative marketing and what is called authentic marketing.

The difference between manipulative and authentic marketing
Authentic book marketing is about presenting a book in front of a person you know has a particular pressing problem/issue, where that person has an interest in solving their problem/issue by reading a book and where the book de facto contains the solution/answer to that person's problem/issue. An important element of authentic

marketing is also that the person in question must have the possibility to choose whether or not to buy the book. When all these criteria are met, you can say that you are doing the person a favor by marketing the book to them. You are offering them a solution and a way forward by giving them the opportunity to buy the book. Authentic marketing will then be perceived as interesting and appealing.

Contrast that with manipulative marketing, which is behind much of the bad reputation that marketing has. Manipulative marketing is about trying to persuade a person to buy something they don't usually want. It tries to take away a person's free will to make the decision for themselves and instead pressure them into buying, which can be perceived as unpleasant and annoying, or sleazy and salesy.

When you focus wholeheartedly on authentic marketing and distance yourself from manipulative marketing strategies, you'll find that marketing doesn't have to be so scary. On the contrary, authentic marketing has all the makings of being creative and fun as its whole purpose is to do your potential customers a favor by promoting a book to them that you know they will want to read.

Amazon's book-savvy customers are always on the lookout for new books

One of my hobbies is reading books. For me, reading is a background activity that I do every day and I try to read all the time when I commute to and from work or have a spare moment between different daily activities. On average, I read for about 45 minutes a day and considering that a book usually takes about five hours to finish, that means I finish a couple of books a month. As a direct consequence of this, like many other avid readers on Amazon, I am constantly on the lookout for new and interesting books to buy.

When you start marketing your book, it's a good idea to have a picture in front of you of how Amazon customers find the books they choose to buy. To explain how this works, I can use myself as an example. I don't think the way I find books is much different from the way the average book-savvy Amazon customer finds their books.

There are many different ways to find new books to read. For example, I regularly scan the top lists in different categories on Amazon, I listen to my favorite authors' podcasts and am influenced by their book recommendations, and I subscribe to Bookbub's daily e-book deals, to name a few ways.

From a marketing perspective, this shows that as a reader, I am constantly on the lookout for new books and that I am usually the one who finds a book I want to read without the author having marketed the book directly to me. If we use this as a general assumption, it means that it is much more often Amazon's customers themselves who find the books they want to read than the other way around, that authors (or publishers) seek out Amazon's customers instead.

In marketing terms, this means that your focus should be on making it easy for Amazon's customers to find your book, rather than you finding Amazon's customers. To kick-start the spiral and make it easy for Amazon's customers to find your book, the first step is to get the right customers to buy the book in the first place.

The right customers must buy your book
After your book has been published and you've checked that the product page looks the way you want it, often the instinct is to want

to get out the megaphone and shout to everyone you know to go in and buy it. But you shouldn't do that quite yet. Instead, my recommendation is that you stay completely quiet and don't tell anyone that the book is out until you've gotten a handful of sales from the right customers. Let me explain why.

If you remember, I wrote in the introduction to this book that Amazon is built around relevance and that the great value of selling books on Amazon is that Amazon itself will do everything it can to market your book for you, provided that they know what your book is about and who it might be of interest to.

Initially, Amazon only has metadata (keywords and categories, etc.) available to make that assessment, but as the book gets more and more sales, the book's product links with other books are strengthened. A product link means that your book will be associated with another book and, for example, will appear on that book's product page in what is called the "customers who have bought have also bought" carousel.

The best long-term marketing strategy is to continually strengthen the product links between your book and other similar books. The effect of this will be that your book will gradually get more and more exposure on Amazon in front of the right readers, as the book will appear on more and more product pages, making it easier for the right customers to find your book, which in turn means more sales.

Another effect of having many customers with similar buying histories and similar book preferences buying your book is that it becomes easier and easier for Amazon to start promoting your book on their own in their emails and around the platform as they have a good idea of who might want to buy the book. This rhymes well with Amazon's business model which is for their customers to have a good buying experience, which largely means exposing them to products that they might actually consider buying.

On several occasions, Amazon's algorithms have picked up some of my books and started marketing them on their own. Of all the different marketing strategies and sales campaigns I've done over the years, I can say that there is no more powerful marketing than having Amazon's algorithms at your back marketing your book for you.

The risk of letting your family or friends buy your book just after it's launched is that their Amazon purchase history is usually not relevant to the book you've published. For example, if a friend of yours reads a lot of fantasy and buys your training book just to be nice, Amazon will think your training book is relevant to those who read fantasy. Then when another of your friends who usually buys children's books buys your exercise book to be nice, Amazon will be confused and not see any clarity in who is buying the book. The effect of this will be that they won't want to display your book in front of their customers as they don't know which customers might be interested in the book. In other words, a marketing effort aimed at the wrong readers can hurt your book's long-term chances of selling, even if in the short term it feels good to get some sales in, of course.

So how do you reach the right customers? There are actually a couple of ways to reach the right customers with fairly simple means. One way is to *hope* that the book will start selling itself, without you actually doing any marketing at all. I'm not a fan of that model. Getting organic sales going is easier after Amazon first learns what your book is about and who it's for.

A better way to get the right customers to buy the book is to pay for ad space, either inside Amazon with Amazon ads, or through a site called Bookbub. The purpose of the advertising is then to expose the book in a few specifically selected places, to start strengthening the links between your book and other similar books. In chapters 11 and 12 I write about how to succeed with Amazon ads and Bookbub ads.

11. Find the right customers using Amazon ads

Amazon has its own advertising service called Amazon ads. Amazon ads is a pay per click (PPC) service, which means that you as an advertiser will only be charged for your ad if one of Amazon's visitors actually clicks on the ad. As an advertiser, you also set your own advertising budget and you decide how much you are willing to pay for each click. This means that if you launch an ad, but none of Amazon's visitors choose to click on it, then it costs you nothing.

As with most things in advertising, not least with Amazon ads, there are several different schools and strategies, some good, some not so good. Of everything I've read about Amazon ads, I think Robert Ryan's book *Amazon Ads Unleashed* and Janet Margot's book *Amazon Ads for Indie Authors* are the two that most closely align with how Amazon ads actually work and how to make the best use of it. If you want a more in-depth look at Amazon Ads than what I write about in this chapter, I recommend reading those books.

What all types of paid advertising have in common, whether it's Amazon ads, Facebook ads, Bookbub ads, or any other advertising service, is that advertising is just the tip of the iceberg when it comes to selling the book. This means that what is below the surface, i.e., the book cover, the title, the book description, the look inside view and the pricing (collectively known as the *packaging* of the book) must also do its part to ensure that those Amazon customers who click on the ad will eventually choose to buy the book.

If the book's packaging is spot on, then advertising can act as rocket fuel for sales. But if the book's packaging is seriously flawed, then it doesn't matter how much money is spent on advertising. The book will never sell anyway.

One advantage of using Amazon ads over other advertising services is that the ad is displayed inside Amazon, in front of a potential customer who has voluntarily surfed to Amazon to look for books. This in turn provides a good opportunity to reach the right customers, which also has a good effect to start strengthening the book product links I wrote about in the previous chapter. Compare this to advertising outside of Amazon, where you have to start by getting the customer to leave a site, such as Facebook, to go to Amazon and then get excited about buying your book. You'll understand that that buying journey is longer and involves more steps.

Amazon ads are constantly evolving with new features and at first glance, launching an ad campaign may seem difficult. I don't think there's any need to complicate the advertising process at this stage and in my opinion, knowing the basics is enough to launch your first successful Amazon ads campaign. The remainder of this chapter can be used as a helping hand for you through the process of launching an Amazon ads campaign for your book.

Launch an Amazon ads campaign

To start with, you need to get into the Amazon ads panel. Go to your KDP account and select "bookshelf". Under "your books" you will see all your books that you have published, where each of them has as its own white box. On the right side of that box, you will see that it says "KINDLE EBOOK ACTIONS" or "PAPERBACK

ACTIONS". Right next to it you will see three dots that you can click on. Click on them and select "promote and advertise". Now a new box will open where you can choose between different ways to promote your book through "KDP Select", "Run a Price Promotion" and "Run an Ad Campaign". In the "Run an Ad Campaign" box, press "choose market-place", select Amazon.com and press the yellow "Create an ad campaign" button.

If everything is correct, you will now be transferred to the Amazon ads panel where you manage everything related to your Amazon ads. Fortunately, you don't have to go the "long" way to Amazon ads every time, once you have started your campaign you can go directly to the website www.advertising.amazon.com.

The first step is to choose the type of ad you want to launch. Amazon changes, adds and removes different types of ads from time to time, but the one that always remains is the one called "sponsored ads". Sponsored ads are Amazon's flagship paid advertising service and the rest of this chapter will therefore focus exclusively on sponsored ads.

The Amazon ads panel
The home screen you see inside Amazon ads is a summary of all your campaigns, both ongoing and completed. In the home screen you will see a graph. If you click on it, you can get statistics on several different parameters from your advertising. You change the parameters by clicking on "add metric" and selecting what you want to see at the moment. Probably it's completely blank there now if you haven't tried your hand at running an Amazon ads campaign before. All metrics are important in their own way and it's possible to dig down and analyze them in great detail, but to keep this on an overall

and reasonably understandable level, there are three metrics in particular that we should learn to keep track of:

1. Impressions

Having the ad displayed inside Amazon is super important. If the ad is not displayed, Amazon's visitors will not be able to click on the ad and without clicks there will be no sales. Even though Amazon ads is built around you as an advertiser only paying when someone clicks on the ad, it is still important that the ad is displayed in the right place in front of the right customer. One trap many people fall into is that they think it shouldn't matter so much where the ad is shown, as you as an advertiser don't pay for the number of views anyway, only for the number of clicks.

As you already know by now, Amazon's business model is to put relevant products in front of the right customers, so that the customer in question has the best possible buying experience. The same reasoning applies very much when it comes to advertising inside Amazon. If you, as an advertiser, contribute to the Amazon customer experience by displaying your ad in relevant places in front of the right customers, then Amazon will give your ad an advantage over other ads that don't deliver on this. For example, such an advantage may mean that Amazon is willing to charge you a lower cost per click compared to what other advertisers are charged.

In the Amazon ads panel, you can see how many impressions the ad has had, and with the amount of traffic Amazon has, it is possible to get many thousands of impressions of an ad *in the right places* every day. When it comes to impressions of the ad, it ultimately boils down to the fact that impressions are still only worth something in a sense as long as they lead to Amazon's visitors actually clicking on the ad as well. Which leads us on to the next metric to check out.

2.   Clicks (number of clicks the ad receives)

Once the ad appears on Amazon, customers need to click on it to go on and buy the book. In your Amazon ads panel, you can see how many clicks an ad gets and how much you've paid for each click. Different Amazon publishing groups have different figures on what counts as a good ratio of impressions to clicks. However, it's hard to generalize and give any exact numbers on this particular one as it varies a lot from niche to niche. However, a good guideline would be one click per 500 impressions. I have good ads that gave a click per 200 impressions but also those that gave a click per 1500 impressions and still gave a successful sales result.

3.   Sales (number of copies sold)

The whole purpose of advertising a book with Amazon ads is for the right customers to find and buy the book. In the Amazon ads panel, you can see how many copies the book has sold thanks to the ad. One myth that is rampant within some Amazon publishing groups is that the sales statistics on the Amazon ads panel don't add up, but they do. The number of copies sold shown inside your Amazon ads panel is the number of sales that are a direct effect of the ad. These will most likely not match your total number of sales that you see during reporting on KDP, which is perfectly fine. This is because Amazon's customers may find and buy your book through other avenues than just your ads, such as through the search feed or when browsing different categories inside Amazon.

The ratio between the number of clicks on the ad and the number of copies sold of the book varies depending on the niche of the book, but as a guideline, with the right packaging and a successful ad, it is possible to achieve about one copy sold for every ten clicks.

Determine your Amazon ads strategy

In Amazon publishing, there is often debate about which is the best Amazon ads strategy. Some argue that it goes without saying that you should advertise for as little money as possible and have as high margins as possible, while others argue that the best strategy is to bid high and try to get as many sales as possible, even if the ad then goes plus/minus zero or even minus. The idea of the latter strategy is that the ad will help to wake up Amazon's algorithms, which will then start to promote the book on their own. In this way, sales of the book can really take off and reach completely different levels than would be possible through advertising alone.

Depending on your budget, how many books you've published and your experience with paid advertising, it's up to you to choose a strategy that you're comfortable with. Maybe you want to try advertising for as little money as possible just because it's fun? Then go for it. Or maybe you've published several books, have previous experience with paid advertising, and are ready to try the plus/minus zero strategy right away? Only you know what suits you best. The important thing to know is that there are different strategies for Amazon ads. Regardless of which strategy you choose, I want to flag that it's hard to make a profit with an Amazon ad if you've only published one book. Even the most established Amazon publishers say that it usually takes at least three books published in a series before you reach the full impact of paid advertising with Amazon ads. I explain why this is so in the section on *publishing in a series* in Chapter 13.

The difference between keyword campaigns and product campaigns

With Amazon sponsored ads, you can make two different types of ads. One targets keywords and the other products. There is a big difference between them and it is not possible to have keywords and products in the same ad campaign. My recommendation is that you try both and see which one works best for you.

Keyword campaign

A keyword campaign is exactly what it sounds like. For example, if you've published a book on yoga for kids, you have the opportunity to buy space in Amazon's feed on various keywords. Let's say you've included the keyword "yoga for kids" as one of the keywords for the book's ad, then the book will appear in the search feed when any of Amazon's customers search for "yoga for kids". Depending on how much you are willing to pay for your ad to appear in the search feed for that keyword, Amazon will charge you different amounts. It usually costs more to appear on page one compared to page five in the search feed.

Product campaign

If you were to launch a product campaign for the yoga for kids book, the ad will not appear in the search feed but will be displayed exclusively on other books' product pages. If you go to a book's product page and scroll down a bit, you will see that there is a sponsored feed of books, which looks basically the same as the "also bought" feed. If you don't see the ad feed, you can try adding a US shipping address to your Amazon account. I've added a Hilton Hotel address as one of my addresses and have that address as the default setting on my Amazon account even though I've never ordered products there. With a US shipping address entered, you will see the

Amazon page reload and the sponsored feed appear. So this is where a product campaign appears in the sponsored feed. This means that these ads will only appear to customers with US shipping addresses.

The advantage of a product campaign is that you can choose which books you want your ad to appear on. In the case of a yoga for kids book, you could have bought ad space on the most popular yoga for kids books, ensuring that the ad appears in front of the right customers.

What determines the book's placement in the ad feed?
As mentioned above, a crucial factor for Amazon ads to work is that the ad is actually displayed inside Amazon. There are several different places where ads can appear, with the majority of all ads appearing either in the search feed or inside the books' product pages.

To the untrained Amazon eye, there is almost no difference between a purchased ad space and a "normal" placement of a book in the feed. If you go to Amazon, select the Kindle Store and type in a keyword, such as "yoga", you will see that the book that appears at the top of the search feed has a small grey text that says "sponsored" just to the right of the cover. The sponsored feed inside the books' product pages will appear in the feed directly below the book description, where you will see that it says "sponsored" in the top left corner of the feed. Remember that a prerequisite for the ads to appear is that you have your Amazon account set to a US shipping address.

As an advertiser, you want your ad to get the best possible ad placement, preferably on the first page of the search feed if you're running a keyword campaign and in the first row of books if you're running a product campaign. These three parameters are the main determinants of where your ad appears in the ad feed:

1.   Bid size

When an Amazon visitor makes a search in the search box or clicks on a product, an automatic auction takes place among all advertisers who have indicated that they are interested in showing their ad for that keyword or inside that product page. Depending on how popular a keyword or product is to advertise on, it costs different amounts of money to win the auction and thus get the best ad placement.

As an advertiser, you decide how much money you are willing to pay to be included in the auction for different keywords and products. This means that if you do not place your ad with high enough bids, your ad will never have a chance to win any auctions, which in turn means that the ad placements your ad can get will not be as numerous and beneficial.

Your advertising strategy and how much you are willing to bid for the ad to win the auctions will therefore determine how much exposure the ad will get. One guideline I have is to always bid at least 50 cents, but occasionally I may be willing to bid up to a dollar per click on some books if I'm trying to kick-start Amazon's algorithms to start marketing and selling the book for me. Here I want to be clear that you shouldn't bid more than you're comfortable spending.

2.   Relevance and clicks

Another parameter that determines where the ad is shown is what Amazon's visitors think about the ad. If they click on the ad, Amazon will want to show it more often compared to other ads that visitors do not click on. Having a good enough ratio between the number of views and the number of clicks is very important for ad placement.

3.   Ad's history

There is a myth in Amazon publishing that Amazon "kills" ads, but they don't. What Amazon does do is give those ads minimal views that do not contribute to a positive customer experience. A positive customer experience in this context means that Amazon's customers find the book interesting enough that they might consider clicking on the ad to further evaluate whether the book is right for them.

In the first period after you launch the ad campaign, both you as an advertiser and Amazon will need to collect data about the ad. This usually takes about two weeks and during that period the ad will appear quite a lot. You should therefore not make any major adjustments to the ad during the first two weeks. After two weeks, it may be a good idea to start optimizing the ad, keeping the keywords or products that generated views and clicks and removing those that did not, so that Amazon gets the sense that you as an advertiser want to contribute to a good customer experience.

As time goes on, Amazon will continue to collect data and get better and better at knowing where the ad is performing best. Therefore, an ad's history can have a big impact on where the ad appears and what ad placement it receives. One way to take advantage of this as an advertiser is to not keep making new campaigns, but rather work on developing an existing ad campaign.

Start a keyword ad:
- Select "sponsored products".
- The first choice you need to make is whether you want your ad to have any ad text or not. I've never found that an

ad text has any direct big impact on how the ad performs, so you can skip the ad text if you want.

- Choose which book you want to advertise (e-book or paperback).
- Select "Manual targeting".
- Select "Keyword targeting".

In the next step, enter the keywords you want your ad to appear on. You will be able to choose "broad", "phrase", or "exact". We can play with the idea that you have published a book on yoga and want to include the keyword "easy yoga for beginners". In the case of "broad", the ad will get impressions on keywords and search phrases that are related to the campaign keywords, even if it's not an exact match. The yoga book in this case would have been displayed if Amazon's customers searched for "easy beginners yoga for adults". In the case of "phrase", the ad is displayed if the Amazon customer searches for the same word as the search phrase, even if the words are placed in a different order. In the case of "exact", the ad will only appear if Amazon's customers search for the exact same word/phrase in the same order as it appears in the ad campaign. My recommendation is that you could try adding both "broad", "phrase" and "exact" to start with and optimize as you get data on what generates views and clicks and what doesn't.

- In "Campaign bidding strategy" I usually choose "down only".
- Finally, you enter a name for the campaign, choose between the dates you want the ad to be active (or if you want it to run without an end date) and set the ad budget. Remember not to advertise for more money than you can afford.

- Press "launch".

Start a product placement ad

Do exactly the same as in the steps above for the keyword ad, but instead of "keyword targeting" choose "product targeting".

Again, a prerequisite for a product placement campaign to work is that it generates views. This in turn requires that the products being advertised are well visited. If you have published a financial book and want to advertise on product pages, the product page for *Rich Dad Poor Dad*, a book that gets thousands of visitors every day, will generate much more exposure than if the ad were to appear on a completely unknown financial book instead.

Sometimes it can be a bit difficult to find good books to target. The winning mindset here is that the visitor who browses to the book you've targeted instead of buying that book, clicks through to your book's ad instead. For this to work, you need to find relevant books to advertise on. One way to do this is to research your book category's top 100 lists and target the ad to books with a sales rank of less than #10,000. Assuming, of course, that those books are relevant and have the same target audience as your book.

To include products in the product placement ad, select:
- "targeting" → "product targeting" → "individual products" → "enter list".
- In the "enter list" box, copy and paste all the ASIN numbers for the relevant targets or search for them in the search box.

Check where the ad is in the feed

Once your ad campaign is approved and the ad has gone live, you can check where the ad appears. If you have made a product placement campaign, go to that product, make sure you have your Amazon account set to a US shipping address and start looking for where the book appears. It usually takes up to 48 hours from the time you launch the ad until it appears. If the ad appears very far back in the ad carousel, you can adjust the bid upwards, wait a few hours and look again to see where it ends up in the carousel. This way you can check that the book is showing as you intended. The same goes for keywords. Try typing in the keyword and see where in the search feed the ad appears. Adjust the bid if you are not satisfied with the ad placement.

Some final thoughts about Amazon ads

Amazon has several different ad platforms, which basically work in the same way. If you have placed an ad on Amazon.com, it will not be visible to customers on Amazon.co.uk. If you want the ad to appear there, you will need to create a separate ad for Amazon.co.uk. Finally, I want to empathise that you should never advertise for more money than you can afford to lose and that you need to be prepared for it to take some time to learn how Amazon ads work. If you want to learn more about this, I again recommend that you read Robert Ryan's and Janet Margot's books that I wrote about at the beginning of this chapter.

12. Find the right customers with the help of Bookbub ads

I wrote earlier that one of the ways I find books for myself is through Bookbub's daily deals. Bookbub (bookbub.com) is the world's largest deal site for e-books. An e-book deal site is a site that connects book lovers with cheap e-books. Bookbub does not sell the e-books themselves, but the daily email contains a link to where the e-book can be purchased, which is usually on Amazon. Subscribing to Bookbub's daily e-books deals is free. The e-books included in Bookbub's emails are usually in the price range of $0.00 (free) to $2.99.

Of all the books I read, about two thirds of them are e-books. The e-book format is becoming increasingly popular and as more readers choose e-books over physical books, many Amazon publishers are also devoting more of their marketing resources exclusively to promoting e-books.

In addition to finding many of the e-books I read in Bookbub's daily deal, I also use paid advertising on Bookbub through Bookbub ads, as a way to launch and promote my own e-books. Bookbub ads offer great opportunities to promote e-books to the right customers and rhyme well with authentic marketing. In this chapter, I explain how you can market your e-book to the right customers using Bookbub ads. I recommend that you start by subscribing to Bookbub yourself to form your own opinion of what you think of their emails. This will also increase your understanding of what Bookbub ads look like and give you some inspiration for designing your own ads.

The design of a Bookbub daily deal email

When you subscribe to Bookbub, you need to choose which categories of e-books and/or specific authors you like to read, so that Bookbub can know which deals to send to whom. Bookbub has millions of subscribers who receive an email in their inbox every day containing today's e-book deals, more or less tailored just for them.

A Bookbub daily deal email has a minimalist look and is designed to draw attention to the book covers of the e-books included in the email. Usually, the email is divided into two parts, the first part containing two or three e-books with so-called feature deals and the second part containing an advertisement, also called a Bookbub ad. Feature deals mean that the author can apply to have his or her e-book included in the email and Bookbub then manually selects the books to be included. Being included in a feature deal on Bookbub can cost up to several thousand dollars for popular categories. The authors or publishers whose e-books are included in Bookbub's daily emails have to pay for it and that's how Bookbub makes its money. I won't go into feature deals any more in this book as I've never managed to get a feature deal on Bookbub myself.

It is the second part of the Bookbub email that is of interest to you as an Amazon publisher. It consists of an advertisement, a Bookbub ad, where you have the opportunity to advertise your e-book without having to apply for it. A Bookbub ad is exposed in the form of a clickable image, i.e., a form of hyperlink to the e-book's product page on Amazon. I'll explain shortly how to get your e-book ad to appear in the email and get Bookbub subscribers to click on the ad.

Bookbub ads and authentic marketing

From an authentic marketing perspective, Bookbub's daily emails are spot on as they land on the doorstep of those who have voluntarily chosen to subscribe to them, which means that everyone who receives the email is guaranteed to be an e-book reader (otherwise they would never have subscribed to Bookbub in the first place!). They have also clicked in that they are interested in reading books in the category that your book is in. If they also open the email, they are most likely also prepared to evaluate whether the e-books in the email are worth buying anyway.

If I try to put myself in the shoes of a Bookbub subscriber, it should go something like this. The email with today's e-book deals arrives and the subscriber enthusiastically opens the email. There is already a certain trust between the subscriber and Bookbub, based on the fact that Bookbub usually presents relevant e-books at a fair price. Let's say that the first two or three books with feature deals did not catch the subscriber's interest, but the subscriber is still eager to buy an e-book and then sees the ad for your e-book exposed directly under feature deals. The ad image is enticing enough for the subscriber to click on it and the subscriber is then transferred to Amazon. Once on Amazon, the subscriber ends up on the e-book's product page and there the packaging of the e-book needs to do its job for the subscriber to buy the book.

Start a Bookbub ads campaign

To get to the panel where you start Bookbub ads, you need to start by opening an account on Bookbub, which is done on Bookbub.com. Once you've done that, click into "Publishers & Authors", which is available at the bottom of the menu bar on Bookbub's home page. Then click on "My promotions" → "Bookbub ads" and finally

"Create an ad". This will take you to the view where you can enter all the information about the ad and make it available to Bookbub's subscribers.

In short, a Bookbub ad consists of three main parts; an ad image, the ad targets (i.e., which Bookbub subscribers the ad will be shown to) and the ad budget. Here I explain in general terms how to hit all three parts right.

The ad image (Ad Creative)

The ad image is very important for the success of a Bookbub ad. It is the one that appears at the end of the Bookbub email. If the ad image is not good enough, the recipients of the email will not click on it. I am by no means a design expert, but of all the different types of ad images I have tested here, an ad image containing the book cover, the deal price and a short interesting text (a few words maximum) has given the most clicks and the best results.

Bookbub subscribers are accustomed to the e-books included in the email being discounted and sold for $0.00-$2.99. But it is possible to use Bookbub to promote e-books that are not discounted as well. When I do a Bookbub ad for an e-book whose normal price is $2.99, I usually use the paperback's price as a reference and then present the $2.99 e-book price as a deal in comparison to the paperback price. In the ad image, I then have the paperback price crossed out and the e-book price prominently displayed next to it, all to reinforce the sense that it's a deal. In this way, it is possible to use Bookbub to promote e-books that are not discounted, but still create the image that the subscriber is getting a deal price.

When I create an ad image, I start by going into the Canva design program (canva.com) and selecting an area that is 300 pixels wide and 250 pixels high, which is the dimension of Bookbub's ad images. Next, I include as large an image of the book cover as possible, the deal price, and a short interesting text. I have posted an example of what this might look like at inkomstmedbocker.se/extra.

My approach to designing ad images for Bookbub ads is by no means the best one, so test out to see what works best for you and your e-books!

Targets (Audience Targeting)

Just like Amazon ads, Bookbub ads need to be displayed in front of the right people who have an interest in buying e-books similar to your e-book. With Bookbub ads, this is done by targeting the ad to specific categories, specific authors or both. Personally, I find that targeting specific authors gives the best results.

When the ad is targeted to an author, it is shown to subscribers who have chosen to follow that author. For example, if you have published a book on marketing and want to reach readers who like to read books on marketing, you can use author targeting to choose that you want the ad to appear in emails that go out to readers who follow, for example, Seth Godin (a popular marketing author).

The important thing when advertising to authors is that the author, or combination of authors (it is possible to include several authors in the same ad), has a sufficient number of followers on Bookbub. One way to check this is to enter the author's name in the Bookbub ads manager and the system will automatically show you how many followers there are of that particular author. When you make a

Bookbub ad, you want to have a total targeting of at least a few thousand people who potentially see the ad. This is so that the ad has the chance to generate enough impressions.

One strategy I usually use to find relevant authors is to start inside Amazon. There I start by selecting a popular book in the same niche as my own e-book and click through to that author's "author page" inside Amazon. Under the author's biography inside the Amazon page, there is usually a collection of other authors under "customers also read book by". Do a quick research on the authors who have published books similar to yours and check how many followers they have on Bookbub, then add more authors until the ad can reach a few thousand of Bookbub's subscribers.

Sometimes it can be tempting to target super-famous authors who have hundreds of thousands of followers just to get the ad in front of a lot of potential customers. Such a strategy can work, but I don't recommend it. In my experience, people who follow the really big authors are not nearly as interested in reading books from "smaller" authors.

Budget and ad auction

The cost of having a Bookbub ad shown in an email varies depending on how many other advertisers are currently looking to have their ads shown in front of the same potential customers as you. The more advertisers bidding on the same targets, the higher the cost of having the ad shown. So, it is the advertisers who drive up the prices. You control how much money you are willing to pay as an advertiser by setting an advertising budget. Bookbub is not ashamed to spend the ad budget and therefore it is important to never enter an amount that you are not comfortable with paying. On the other hand, it is important not to have too small a budget, because then the ad will not win any bid auctions and therefore will not be shown to any potential customers.

When you set up the ad, you will see that Bookbub shows a range of how much money most winning bidders usually bid. My strategy is to always bid slightly higher than what the range shows. The ad budget and the actual cost you end up paying are not always the same thing. If five advertisers are bidding at the top of Bookbub's range, say $10, but you instead indicate that you want an ad bid of $11. What happens then? When the bid auction starts, you will win the bid auction because you bid the highest. The amount you are charged will be $10.01 and not $11. Why this is so has to do with the fact that the budget controls the maximum amount of money you are willing to spend, but the cost you are actually charged is only one cent over the "runner-up" in the bid auction.

An important choice when it comes to the ad budget is whether Bookbub should spend the budget as quickly as possible or whether they should spread it over the number of days you have chosen to have the ad running. The first time you run a Bookbub ad, my recommendation is that you spread the budget over two or three days.

Two different strategies to reach the right customers
When you make a Bookbub ads campaign, you can choose to display your ad in two different ways. One way is CPC (cost per click) and the other is CPM (cost per 1,000 impressions). The difference between them is significant. In a CPC campaign, you only pay when someone clicks on the ad image, whereas in a CPM campaign, you

pay for when the ad appears, regardless of whether someone clicks on the ad image or not.

Personally, I prefer CPM campaigns because I have the ability to control the budget so that the ad is guaranteed to appear by bidding high enough to win the bidding auction. Once the ad appears, it's up to me to make sure I've made a really good ad image and targeted the ad to the right customers so that the ad will generate clicks to the book's product page on Amazon. So with a CPM campaign, I can have a greater impact on how many people click on the ad by targeting the ad to the right authors and having an ad image that the target audience actually clicks on.

We can take a numerical example to show how it works in practice. Let's say I'm willing to pay $15 for 1,000 impressions and I manage to get 35 people to click on the ad. Then I pay 42 cents per click ($15/35 clicks). If instead I manage to make an ad image so attractive that 60 people click on it instead, then I only pay 25 cents per click ($15/60 clicks). If, on the other hand, I'm running a CPC campaign, it's common to have to pay up to 70 cents per click to be guaranteed to win the bidding auction that determines which ad to display.

The type of campaign you prefer is up to you. What works for me may not always work for you. Test out which type (CPC or CPM) works best for you and your e-books.

Behind the scenes of a Bookbub campaign that generated hundreds of sales

When I launched my book Likes Don't Pay Bills, I did so under a completely new author name. I had no social media and no website, but thanks to Bookbub ads, I was able to boost sales and sell hundreds of e-books in the launch month alone.

Before I invested in Bookbub ads, I did an Amazon ad to make sure there were no flaws in the packaging of the book. Amazon ads provide a slightly different type of data than Bookbub ads, which makes it easier to track whether those who click on the ad actually buy the book or not. With Amazon ads, you can instantly see how many impressions, how many people click on the ad and how many people buy the book. When I had proof that the whole chain impressions->clicks->sales was sufficiently optimized and targeted, I made a couple of Bookbub ads with different ad images and different targets to test which combination gave the lowest click cost and best results.

Remember that in a CPM campaign on Bookbub you pay for the number of impressions, so you need to test the combination of ad image and targeting to see if readers click on the image enough before you spend the big bucks. When I found a combination that I thought was good enough at the time (more than 2% who saw the ad clicked on it), I gradually increased the budget to make the ad generate more impressions.

Gradually, I increased the budget and tried to get more and more impressions, which in turn brought more clicks and more sales. On inkomstmedbocker.com/extra I have posted a screenshot showing how I tried to increase sales step by step in the hope that Amazon would pick up the e-book and start recommending it on their own. It succeeded in a way in that Amazon chose to keep the price of the e-book at $0.99 for a month after my Bookbub ads campaign ended even though I raised the price of the e-book myself to $2.99 and received royalties as if the e-book cost $2.99. Amazon thus chose to temporarily lose money on selling my e-book in order to offer their customers a good deal, which is perfectly in line with their strategy of giving customers what they want and thereby increasing trust between them and the platform.

Final thoughts about Bookbub ads

For me, Bookbub ads have a central place in my marketing campaigns and I highly recommend that you try Bookbub ads for yourself. If you are running a CPM campaign where you pay for the number of views, it will make high demands on the ad image and targeting. One last tip when it comes to Bookbub ads is that in addition to advertising to the US, you can advertise to both the UK and Canada. This is easily done by going to English Amazon (Amazon.co.uk) and Canadian Amazon (Amazon.ca) and including the .co.uk hyperlink and the .ca hyperlink to your e-book in the Bookbub ads manager.

13. How to scale up and increase book sales

One of the reasons why many are interested in testing Amazon publishing is because the whole structure and business model around Amazon publishing is scalable. The scalability of a business model means that there is no linear relationship between how many hours you work and how much money you make. In this way, scalable business models have the potential to generate more and more revenue without the time investment increasing to the same extent.

Scalable business models can have an almost seductive aura about them and it's easy to fall into the trap of thinking that you don't need to invest any time at all to succeed in making money, which of course isn't really true. On the contrary, scalable business models often take more time to get off the ground than you might think, but it is usually well worth the effort.

The scalable impact of Amazon publishing comes from the fact that Amazon customers can find and buy your book, without you, the publisher, having to be present for every transaction. Instead, you can spend time developing new books, offering Amazon customers even more books to buy, which will increase your revenue in the long run.

The way Amazon publishing is structured, there is every opportunity to scale up revenue without increasing time investment. However, a prerequisite for doing so is that you have proof that Amazon customers actually buy your book.

Once you have proof that Amazon customers are buying your book, then you can turn your attention to scaling up revenue. The Amazon publishers who have managed to scale up their revenues and make really good money from their books, but have also been generous enough to tell us how they did it, have several things in common that I want to highlight in this chapter. But first, let's look at some things you can do if your published book isn't selling.

Troubleshooting if your book doesn't sell despite authentic marketing

Few things can be as frustrating as putting time, money and energy into publishing a book and then being met with the silence of the book not selling. Before I describe how you can troubleshoot and repair the error to get sales going, I just want to be clear that there is a big difference between a book selling a few copies here and there versus a book selling nothing at all. If your book sells a few copies here and there, that's proof enough that Amazon's customers are actually buying the book. But if the book doesn't sell at all, then the fault probably lies in one of these three parts:

1) The book cover and title do not attract the right customers

It's a cliché to say that you shouldn't judge a book by its cover, but that's exactly what most people do! The cover needs to clearly signal the book's niche and look professional to attract the attention of the right customers. If it doesn't, then sales are downhill from the start.

If your book isn't selling and you think it might have something to do with the cover, my recommendation is to change the cover as soon as you can. Several times my books have started selling steadily every week after I update a cover for a book that wasn't selling before.

2) The product page does not make customers want to buy the book

Let's say the fault is not in the book cover, which you can know if you do paid advertising and the ad generates clicks to the book's product page, but the book still doesn't sell. In that case, there is almost certainly one or more flaws on the book's product page.

What you can do then is to make sure that the price of the book is in line with other similar books, that the book description makes a clear promise to the reader of what the reader will get out of reading the book and that the "look inside" view answers the promised promise in a sufficiently interesting way.

3) Wrong or too little traffic to the book

A common misconception about a book not selling is that it must mean there is not enough traffic to it. That may be so, but more often than not I would argue that the reason a book doesn't sell really has nothing to do with the traffic to the book.

The truth is that trying to boost sales by increasing traffic to the book alone does not help at all unless the book cover and product page do their job. On the contrary, more traffic to a book that is not selling can make the problem worse by feeding Amazon more data that their customers are not interested in buying the book.

However, if it is indeed the case that a book is not selling because of too little traffic, it is a relatively easy problem to solve by reviewing the book's metadata (keywords, categories, etc.) and spending money on traffic-generating ads such as Amazon ads or Bookbub ads.

Last resort - republish the book

If sales do not take off despite all attempts to correct any errors, the last resort is to republish the book completely, with a new title, cover and description. If you have only published an e-book, you can republish the e-book in its entirety without unpublishing the old one, but if you have published both an e-book and a paperback, you must unpublish both the e-book and the paperback before republishing them. The reason why you have to unpublish the paperback is because Amazon locks the title, subtitle and author name of the paperback after it goes live.

Unpublishing a book is easy. Go to your KDP account, tap on Bookshelf and look on the far right within the book's box under "your books". There are three dots. Hover over them, at the bottom it says "unpublish book".

I have a rule for myself before I take the step of republishing a book. It is that I must first have made a proper attempt to get the book to start selling. If the book doesn't sell, it's rarely the fault of the content of the book, but 99 times out of 100 it's because the packaging (the title, subtitle, book cover, book description and "look inside") doesn't appeal to the intended audience.

Before republishing a book, I recommend that you spend some time analyzing what part of the packaging chain is lacking and make a plan of what you need to fix and how to do it.

Put yourself in the shoes of an Amazon customer and think about; is the cover appealing enough to capture the interest of the intended audience and make them curious to know more about the book? If the answer to that question is yes, then what is it about the book description or "look inside" that makes them not buy the book anyway? It could be, for example, that the book description is perceived as cluttered or manipulative or that the "look inside" view is not interesting enough.

Reposting can have a good effect. At one point when I was coaching someone who was publishing books in relationship niche, we were having trouble getting the book titled "Solo Mom Finds: How to get your ex back fast" off the ground. At the time, the book had a cover that didn't clearly signal nonfiction, so readers had a hard time knowing whether it was a fiction book or a nonfiction book. After we republished the book with the title "Get Him Back" and made the cover like any other relationship book cover in the niche, sales took off immediately. Exactly the same content in the book but the packaging was completely different. Clarity in the packaging of the book is often the key to getting sales going.

Scale up by owning the connection with your customers and followers

One of the most valuable assets you can have as a seller, whether you're selling books on Amazon, selling skincare products in your own online store or running a restaurant, is that you own the connection with your customers and followers. Owning the contact with your customers and followers can be achieved in different ways, the most common being having them gathered in an email list. Now you may be thinking that email sounds old fashioned and boring, but it doesn't have to be. Email can be rockin'!

Having your customers and followers in an email list makes a significant difference compared to only having contact with your customers and followers on one of the major social media platforms, as many salespeople have today. On social media, you more or less rent the opportunity to reach your customers and followers and you don't own the relationship with them in the same way. Let's say you have all your customers and followers on Instagram. Since Instagram owns their platform and can decide on it themselves, they can close your account or change their terms at any time so that you can't reach your customers. If you have your customers and followers in an email list, you are the one who owns the relationship with them and you are not dependent on any other party to sell your products and services.

As an Amazon publisher, an email list is most effective if the people who have signed up to the list have a genuine interest in reading books in the same niche as you publish in. With an email list filled with people who have that interest, you can expect them to open your emails and actually want to know what you have to say. A setup that rhymes well with authentic marketing.

The challenge with an email list is to get just the right people to sign up to it, which in theory is relatively easy to achieve. Theoretically, the simplest strategy, if you can even call it a strategy, is not to focus on it at all. Instead, it's better to put all the effort and energy into selling as many copies of the book as possible and let the book's end/final words do the work of capturing the right people and leading them on to sign up to the mailing list. When it's up to the end of the book to do the work of capturing the right people for the email list, it means that the more people who buy the book, the more people are likely to sign up for the email list. With such a strategy, all the focus is on making the book as accessible to the right customers as possible and getting as many people as possible to buy and read the book.

While this is a simple strategy that will certainly fill your email list with people who have actually read the book and want to hear more from you, it is entirely dependent on you selling a lot of books because the majority of people who read the book and think it's good won't sign up for the email list anyway. Therefore, it might be a good idea to have another complementary strategy close at hand.

One way to get more people to sign up to the mailing list is to offer something in return for signing up. In email marketing, this is usually referred to as offering a "freebie" or "lead magnet". A freebie or lead magnet aims to increase the incentive to subscribe to the email list by directly providing something of value in exchange for a person's e-mail address. There are different approaches as to which type of freebie or lead magnet is best. I think an appropriate freebie is some type of short e-book that addresses the same pressing issue that you have based your book on. That way you know that those who sign up for the email list and take advantage of the freebie are most likely also interested in reading your book.

In addition to letting readers find the link to the freebie at the end of the book, you can also use social media to drive traffic to the freebie. Then, with relatively simple means, you can use a platform like Instagram in order to get followers who then sign up to your email list. The purpose of Instagram in this case is then to use Instagram as a traffic source.

How to increase revenue with an email list
Once you've started to fill your email list with the right people, the next challenge begins: selling in email! One way to succeed in email selling is not to sell all the time, but to mix up the selling with regular

interesting and value-adding emails where you don't expect anything back from those who open and read your emails. A common ratio of selling to non-selling is usually 20% selling and 80% non-selling, but I don't think that's set in stone. You can test it out and see what works best for you.

The challenge of running an email list is to constantly have something of value to share, so that those who receive your emails find it worthwhile to open and read them. Personally, I think there is far too little talk about how to constantly have valuable and interesting topics to share. In my view, it's hard to write value-adding and interesting emails from a vacuum. By that I mean it requires you as a person to actively work to find interesting topics that you can package and share in your unique way. My best tip when it comes to finding interesting topics is to read books. As I wrote earlier, I read about 45 minutes a day and in addition to reading being a hobby, it helps me to constantly expose myself to new ideas, which contribute to new insights and new connections between different topics. I make frequent use of these when writing emails to my various email lists.

Another important part of email marketing is that you should send out emails at regular intervals, so that those who have signed up for your list don't forget who you are. My recommendation is to send out at least once a month, but preferably more often if you can.

When I coach in Amazon publishing, I always push to start an email list as early in the process as possible, and I want to give the same encouragement to you. Start an email list as soon as you have proof that your book is selling! Then, when you publish your second book, you'll quickly see the value of having an email list. Using the email list will also allow you to reach out and ask for a review of your book at launch.

Publishing two or more books in a series

Once you have proof that Amazon customers are buying your book and you have a system for capturing your customers and followers in an email list, you have everything you need to successfully scale your Amazon publishing business.

A common denominator for virtually everyone who has managed to scale up sales on Amazon is that they have published multiple books in the same niche. When you have published at least two books in the same niche, you can make a series page inside Amazon. A series page is a page where all the books in the series are listed and from there Amazon customers can buy all the books in the series with a single click. The series name is also searchable, which means you can include keywords in the series name, which in turn gives your books even more exposure inside Amazon. In other words, series pages can be rocket fuel for sales!

In addition to being able to do series pages, the ability to offer more than one book to the customers means completely different mathematics if you do paid advertising. To demonstrate this, I'll compare two scenarios, the first based on having published one book and the second based on having published three books.

Scenario 1:

Say you sell a standalone e-book for $4.99 with a 70% royalty. For each copy sold, you get $3.49 ($4.99 x 0.7). If you do paid advertising and you sell an e-book to every tenth person who clicks on the ad, the ad goes plus/minus zero at the bid level of $0.349 per click

($0.349 x 10 = $3.49). If you recall from the chapter on Amazon ads, it's hard to win any bid auctions if you don't bid high enough. This applies to both keyword campaigns and product campaigns. If the limit for the ad to go plus/minus zero is at $0.349 per click, it's hard to get the ad to win the bid auction, which limits the possibilities of getting impressions, which in turn limits how many copies of the e-book can potentially be sold.

Scenario 2:

Instead, say you have published three e-books, all three of which are in the same niche and target the same potential customer. Again, the e-books cost $4.99 each and you receive 70% royalties equivalent to $3.49 per copy sold. In this case, you have a completely different equation to make paid advertising profitable.

If you advertise book one in the series and for every reader who buys book one, you know that half of them will also buy book two for $4.99 and of those who buy book two, half will also buy book three for $4.99. If you then sell 100 copies of book one, you know that you will sell 50 copies of book two and 25 copies of book three. The value of selling one book through the ad is then (($4.99 x 70%) + 0.5($4.99 x 70%) + 0.25($4.99 x 70%)) = $6.11. Still, one in ten people who click on the ad buys the book, but knowing that you will ultimately earn $6.11 per book sold, you can now pay $0.61 per click, instead of $0.349, without going broke on the ad. With such a significantly higher tolerance, you can bid higher, win more bid auctions and get more impressions on the ad. So, publishing multiple books in a series makes it easier for you to make money from your paid advertising.

Author profile

On Amazon, you have the option to create an author profile page where you can write a biography of the author, add a photo and have all the author's books listed. Creating an author page works equally well whether you have published your book under your own name or under a fictitious pseudonym. If you go to Amazon and click on one of your favorite authors, you can see what an author page looks like. You can easily create your own author page by going to www.authorcentral.amazon.com and following the instructions there.

The core of the author page is the image and the text. If you have published your book under your own name, you can include a picture of yourself and if you have published your book under a pseudonym, you can use a stock photo from Shutterstock.com or something similar.

When writing the author bio, put yourself in the readers' perspective and think about what they want to know. Most likely, they want to know what they will get out of reading your books, so focus on communicating that. One mistake many people make, in my opinion, is that they only write about themselves. Sure, it's an "about" page, but isn't it a bit boring to read a half-bragging "about" pages? Instead, I think you should use the author bio on the author's page as a way to build trust with readers and reinforce the image that you are the right person to publish the book.

Increase traffic and test new marketing approaches

Increasing traffic to the books is a key part of scaling up, but as I've written about before, it only works if all the pieces of the book's packaging are in just the right place. In addition to using Amazon ads and Bookbub ads to drive traffic, many Amazon publishers are diligent about promoting their books on social media.

Social media can work to drive traffic to books, but it can also be a real time-sink. I rarely recommend social media marketing in Amazon publishing. The reason for this is that many people who use social media are completely uninterested in reading books, and as a marketer it's easy to fall into the trap of trying to amass large followings in the hope that the number of followers is what counts. What risks happening then is that a lot of time is spent building up a following that may not actually have an interest in buying your books on Amazon.

If you do want to give social media a go, the strategy for success is basically the same as for any authentic marketing. Your followers need to be the focus and you, the marketer, need to give them something they want, and then lead them to buy your book. And remember, you only want followers who are actually interested in what you have to offer!

Other ways to increase traffic include a website, YouTube, or being part of a podcast. However, at some point there is a limit to what an Amazon publisher can do on their own to increase traffic to their books. Big traffic increases come mainly from other people starting to recommend your books to their friends and followers.

Final thoughts about scaling up
To my knowledge, there are no shortcuts or secrets when it comes to scaling up. Take it one step at a time and start by getting your book selling with Amazon ads and Bookbub ads before moving on to other more advanced marketing methods.

As you may have noticed, I haven't written anything about how to get reviews on a book, other than that you can use the end/final words of the book and also use your email list to ask for reviews. But the email list only becomes relevant after you have launched the book, so how do you go about getting reviews on the book quickly? The best way to get reviews for a book is to package the book in a professional way, market the book to the right customers, and have patience. Assuming the book then answers readers' most pressing questions, the reviews will start to roll in automatically.

To conclude, I would also like to say that reviews are something that many Amazon publishers focus on and the reasoning is that more reviews automatically lead to more sales. In my experience, this does not have to be the case. Sure, it helps sales if the book has a few reviews, but more reviews does not guarantee increased sales. The best way to scale up is to publish more books in the same series, package them in a professional way and market them to the right customers.

14. Low content publishing

A growing trend in Amazon publishing is to publish low content books. Low content is defined as books without, or with limited, textual content. Typical of low content are various types of activity books. For example, an activity book can be a coloring book, a crossword puzzle book, a sudoku book, a notebook, a diary or a planning book. If you browse around on Amazon, you'll soon find that there are lots of low content books on just about everything and then some.

A few years ago, hardly any Amazon publishers were talking about low content, but now it's on many people's lips. Why is that? A big reason why low content has gained such a huge following among Amazon publishers is because of the relatively small start-up costs compared to hiring a ghostwriter and producing a "regular" book. In addition to low start-up costs, low-content books can be brought to market quickly because they are often produced from a variety of ready-made templates. This means that it is possible to publish a large number of low content books quickly at a low cost, which means that it is possible to quickly build up a portfolio of books that have the potential to generate that coveted passive income that most of us Amazon publishers crave.

Low content publishing has grown exponentially and there are those who have published as many as thousands of low content books in an attempt to cash in on the growing demand for activity books. To do this, I know of those who have been so ingenious as to create a document with 200 lined pages, slap on a homemade book cover and publish it as a "notebook". Can you really do that, you might think, and does anyone really buy such a book? Yes, you can. And yes, it sells.

I've been following the development of low content for some time and in 2021 I felt it was time to try publishing some low content books myself to form my own opinion of whether, and how, low content publishing works. This chapter is a small case study of what I've learned so far about publishing low content books.

Advantages and disadvantages of low content

I think the biggest advantages of low content are definitely the start-up costs and the time. You can go from book idea to finished book in just a few days and only spend a fraction of the money compared to what it costs to publish a regular book.

The downside is that virtually all low-content books can only be sold as physical books. This means that the entire e-book and audiobook market is out of reach, a major disadvantage as digital book formats grow year on year and turn over more and more. Not being able to have a book published also as an e-book also means that a number of marketing platforms such as Bookbub, which only targets digital books, play out their role completely. As a publisher, you are then almost entirely dependent on Amazon ads to reach the right customers.

Choosing the right low content niche

Amazon makes no distinction between a regular physical book and a low content book. This means that all physical books sold on Amazon are included in the same ranking. You can therefore analyse the best seller ranking in the same way as for other books to get an indication of whether a certain type of low content book is selling or not. If you've forgotten how to find the best seller ranking, here's a little refresher. Go to any low content book, scroll down to "Product details" and there read off the ranking in "Best seller rank in books". If you see a ranking of #100,000 or lower (better), that means you've found a book that sells at least a few copies a week. Using best seller ranks, you can then investigate whether or not multiple books in a particular low content niche are selling and thus choose to move forward with producing the type of low content book that you know Amazon's customers are actually buying.

Lessons from my low content books

Once I decided to try low content publishing, the first thing I did was watch YouTube clips and listen to other Amazon publishers who publish a lot of low content. Pretty early on, it became clear that most of the low content publishers had one thing in common. They talked about the importance of finding a "hot" niche with a seemingly small supply combined with high demand.

In theory this is a brilliant strategy, but from experience I know that the reality on Amazon is different. The "hot" smaller niches with high demand are hard to find, if they even exist. After all, for those who want to sell a lot of books and make a lot of money, it is better to try to break into the larger more commercial niches.

It is easy to see that the smaller niches do not generate as much traffic and do not sell as many books. Just look at the best seller ranks of several books in the different top 100 categories to see which of all categories is the one that sells the most books.

Speaking of smaller niches, let me make it clear that I have nothing against smaller niches. A smaller niche can serve a clear purpose if it is to learn the publishing process and develop one's skills in Amazon publishing, in order to eventually break into larger niches with more potential. When choosing the low content niche, I decided not to look for a "hot" small niche but instead turn my eyes towards the larger niches, as I felt confident that the knowledge I have about Amazon and Amazon ads would help me to at least have a chance of breaking in there.

After doing research in several different niches, it was finally a choice between publishing coloring books or sudoku books. The scales finally tipped in favor of sudoku books, partly because they seemed easier to produce and partly because sudoku books are a very special type of book that only attracts those who are really interested in sudoku. This means that the buying journey for a sudoku customer does not include as many evaluation moments as for those looking for other types of books. In any case, one Sudoku puzzle may not be that much different from another, apart from the level of difficulty. If a customer wants to buy a Sudoku book, then it is a Sudoku book the customer wants to buy. If, on the other hand, a customer is looking for a coloring book, it may be that it has to be a coloring book with certain special motifs, which means that the buying journey contains more considerations that may affect the sale.

Writing to market for low content
Producing a low content book, no matter what low content niche you choose to publish in, has a lot in common with producing a nonfiction book. Even if a low content book contains limited text, you still need to see the book from the customer's perspective and be sure that the book delivers what the customer expects. Questions such as, *Does the book provide value to the reader? What does the reader want to get out of the book? How will the book deliver that?* are just as important

in low content, and the concept of writing to market is very relevant here too.

On Amazon, there are tens of thousands of reviews on various low content books. When I was making my sudoku books, I started by reviewing the reviews of the best-selling sudoku books. It only took me an hour to get enough information on my feet to know what was good (or not so good) about several of the best-selling sudoku books on Amazon. As an example, a consistent comment in many reviews was that customers complained that the squares in many of the sudoku books were too small, resulting in not enough room to write mistakes, or barely any room to write at all. When I felt I knew what the sudoku market wanted, I bought a computer program that automatically generates sudoku puzzles and started making three sudoku books.

How to find content for low content books
There are several ways to develop the content for a low content book. Depending on the low content niche you have chosen, you can buy a program that generates the content for the books, like I did for my sudoku books, or you can buy ready-made templates from fiverr.com or etsy.com, for example. If you choose to buy a template, just be sure that you have the right to actually publish the template on Amazon. Another option is to design and produce the content of your low content book yourself.

Packaging a low content book
The strategy to succeed in selling low content books is exactly the same as for non-fiction. A prerequisite for having a chance of selling low content books is that Amazon's customers are somehow attracted to the book by the cover signaling the right message. Then

the product page with the book description and "look inside" must do its job to get the customer to buy the book. This means that just because it is "easier" to produce a low content book, it does not mean that the packaging of the book is easier or less important.

Publish your low content book the right way
Publishing low content books is exactly the same as publishing paperbacks on KDP. This means that all metadata must be relevant and you can add up to ten categories to your low content book as well. The pricing of the book should match other books in the niche, possibly marginally higher to cover the advertising costs that are basically a must to boost sales.

Boost low content sales
Even when it comes to selling low-content, Amazon works to sell the right book to the right customer. You can go back through the book and read about everything from how Amazon's algorithms work, to different Amazon ads strategies, to what you can do to scale up sales. All of this is directly applicable to low content as well.

Results from my Sudoku books
So how did my sudoku books do? In all honesty, not very good. In 2021, they generated $2,500 in royalties after $1,500 in advertising costs, which is a testament to the fact that as a low content publisher, it can be difficult to get sales going and you are relatively dependent on paid advertising to successfully sell your books.

In terms of content, however, customers seem reasonably satisfied. The books have received overwhelmingly positive reviews, but I am convinced that it is certainly possible to produce much better Sudoku books than my computer program is capable of.

Overall, I'm still happy with my low content test and I recommend you also try low content publishing if you want to get started quickly with trying to publish your own book on Amazon!

Get Amazon Income for FREE on Audible

I'm giving away free Audible copies of this book.

Get your free coupon codes (value $19.99) when you sign up for the email list at www.inkomstmedbocker.se/english

Connect with the author

Of all the books to choose from, I want to thank you very much for choosing *Amazon Income* and reading all the way to the end.

In the introduction, I wrote that my goal with this book is to give you the information you need to produce, publish, and market books on Amazon that Amazon's customers want to pay for and that can generate income for you each month.

Do you think the book has lived up to that?

If you think the book has lived up to your expectations (or more) then you are very welcome to write that in a review. Likewise, if you thought the book only contained things that you could have easily Googled or found on YouTube, then I'd love to know that too!

For those who want to know even more about Amazon publishing, get an insight into the latest trends and marketing strategies, but also much more about succeeding with your books on Amazon, I recommend signing up for my free weekly article. There I also share a deeper insight into my books and how I am constantly developing my own book business.

Get the weekly article at www.inkomstmedbocker.se/english.

Finally, I want to thank you again for reading this book and wish you the best of luck with your own books!

Christian Öberg

Contact:
Web: inkomstmedbocker.se/english
Email: christian@inkomstmedbocker.se
Instagram: @inkomstmedbocker

1:1-coachingprogram

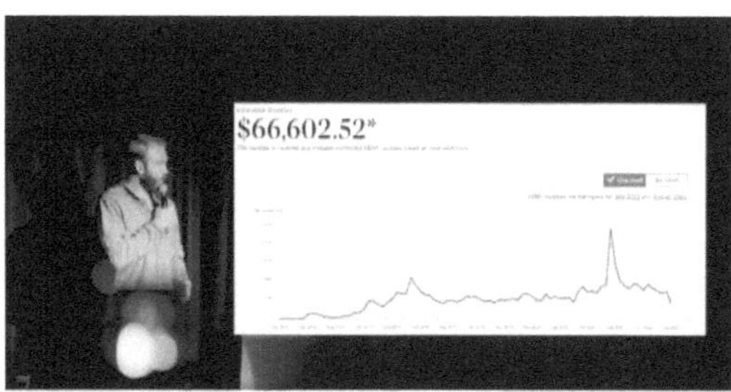

RESULT: You will learn how to produce, publish and market books on Amazon that can generate income for you every month for a long time to come.

BEHIND THE SCENES: You'll learn the strategies I personally use to earn $2,500/month, including how to get started selling audiobooks on Amazon (a booming market with little competition).

6 SESSIONS: We meet on Zoom at a time that suits you. Each session is one hour, and a reasonable pace is about one session every two weeks.

TRY-ON SESSION: It's great to try a session before you decide to buy a coaching package. The try-on session is about finding the right book idea for you. The try-on session is 45 minutes. It does not count as an session in the coaching package.

PRICE (incl. VAT): 6 sessions: $899 US. Try-on session: $99 US.

Do you want to buy a coaching package or a try-on session?

Book a time for your first session in the booking calendar at inkomstmedbocker.se/english or email me at christian@inkomstmedbocker.se

9 789919 868140 6